Access 2002 VBA

Programming Access

Published by :

FIREWALL MEDIA

(An Imprint of Laxmi Publications Pvt. Ltd.)
113, Golden House, Daryaganj,
New Delhi-110002

Phone : 011-43 53 25 00
Fax : 011-43 53 25 28

www.laxmipublications.com
info@laxmipublications.com

Economy Edition Price : **Rs. 295.00** *Only.* *Edition* : 2008

OFFICES

India

© **Bangalore**	080-26 61 15 61
© **Chennai**	044-24 34 47 26
© **Cochin**	0484-239 70 04
© **Guwahati**	0361-254 36 69, 251 38 81
© **Hyderabad**	040-24 65 23 33
© **Jalandhar**	0181-222 12 72
© **Kolkata**	033-22 27 43 84
© **Lucknow**	0522-220 95 78
© **Mumbai**	022-24 91 54 15, 24 92 78 69
© **Ranchi**	0651-221 47 64

USA

Boston
11, Leavitt Street, Hingham,
MA 02043, USA

FIT-2732-295-IT RES ACCESS 2002 VBA PROG
ISBN : 81-7008-475-X

C—15841/08/05
Printed at : Sanjeev Offset Printers, Delhi.

Overview

Chapter 1

Visual Basic language

Chapter 2

Objects and collections Chapter 3

Data access objects Chapter 4

SQL language Chapter 5

Managing events Chapter 6

Debugging and managing errors Chapter 7

Customizing forms and reports Chapter 8

Customizing the user interface — Chapter 9

Communicating with other Office XP applications — Chapter 10

Internet programming — Chapter 11

Windows programming — Chapter 12

Example of a mini-application Chapter 13

Appendices

The Access 2002 VBA (Visual Basic for Applications) programming language allows you to extend Access' features and get the most out of this application.

VBA is both a powerful language and one that beginners find easy to use and understand. VBA is largely based on Visual Basic, with specific statements (objects, methods, function, etc.) that allow you to handle Access objects.

You can program Access 2002 in two ways:

- visual programming: using the application interface (forms and reports).
- underlying programming: using DAO (Database Access Objects) with the Microsoft Jet 4.0 database engine.

To get the most out of this book, you must have used Access 2002 and be able to create, change, delete and handle tables, queries, forms, data access pages and reports. You must also have a general knowledge of programming techniques.

Chapter 1: Overview

A. Definitions

An Access database is composed of a single file with an .mbe or .mde name extension (mde format hides the database's Visual Basic code and does not allow you to change its forms or its reports). This database file contains the different objects of the application. Here are the different types of object:

Tables

Database tables contain data and can be linked together.

Queries

Queries allow you to:

- select and sort tables,
- make simple calculations and crosstab analyses,
- carry out actions (such as creating tables and adding, deleting and updating records),
- run SQL operations.

Forms

Forms allow you to enter and update data.

Reports

Reports allow you to print all sorts of database information, from simple reports of table contents to complex reports that group records and make calculations.

Data access pages

Data access pages are used to publish database information rapidly on an intranet or the Internet.

Macros

A macro allows you to automate a set of tasks using a specific language. However, macros do not offer the development power of VBA.

Modules

Modules contain specific parts of the VBA code, such as declarations, functions and procedures.

B. Basic concepts

VBA provides an object oriented programming environment.

An object is an independent entity that uses certain data (such as its properties: size, color and value, for example) and acts in a certain way (according to its methods, for example). You can access some objects using visual interfaces (such as Forms and Reports) while you must use VBA code to access other objects (such as DBEngine and Container).

Most visual objects can act upon events (on opening or after modification, for example).

VBA programming allows you to define specific object actions upon certain events. This involves defining specific methods, procedures and functions in the VBA code. As it involves a modular approach, this technique helps you to write better code. In addition, it provides flexibility and ease of maintenance.

Object structure

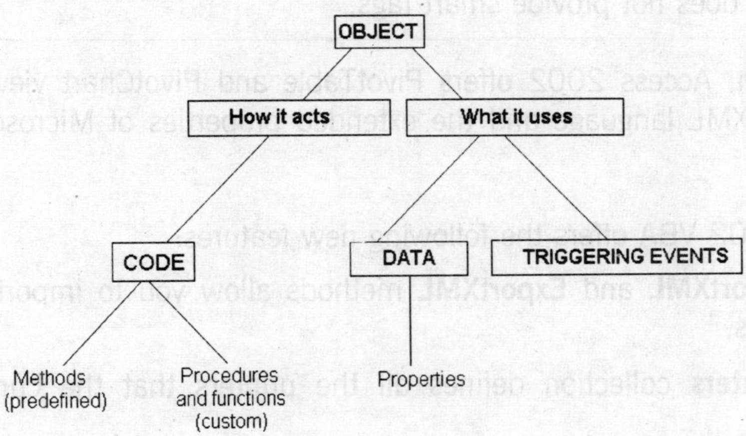

Event — a user or system action that triggers corresponding object code.

Method — predefined code for a type of object.

Procedure — a sequence of statements that does not return a value.

Function — a sequence of statements that returns a value.

C. What is new with Access 2002

Access 2002 is part of the **Microsoft Office XP** (eXPerience) suite and benefits from most of the improvements that this Office version offers. It provides a simple, easy-to-understand interface with task panes, and access to the answer wizard directly from the **Ask a Question** box in the menu bar.

Access does not provide smart tags.

In addition, Access 2002 offers PivotTable and PivotChart views and supports the XML language and the extended properties of Microsoft SQL Server 2000.

Access 2002 VBA offers the following new features:

- the **ImportXML** and **ExportXML** methods allow you to import and export XML files,
- the **Printers** collection defines all the printers that the current system provides,
- the **AllFunctions** collection groups all the user functions for a Microsoft SQL Server 2000 database,

- the **Move** method allows you to move a control in a form or a report,
- the **Form** object offers **new events** concerning PivotTables, PivotCharts and transactions, etc.

D.Upgrading from macros to VBA

Macros provide an easy means of implementing a sequence of simple actions, such as opening and closing forms.

However, VBA offers other advantages:

- it helps you to maintain your databases, as it allows you to use Visual Basic event procedures to define your forms and reports,
- it provides enhanced error management,
- it can carry out actions at system level,
- it allows you to handle one record at a time,
- it can pass arguments to the VBA code that is currently running,
- it supports automatic conversion of any macro into VBA code.

Converting macros on a form or report

→ Open the form or report in Design view, select the **Tools - Macro** menu option and choose **Convert Form's Macros to Visual Basic** or **Convert Report's Macros to Visual Basic**.

Converting global macros

➔ In the **Objects** bar of the database window, choose the **Macros** option.

➔ Select the **File - Save As** menu option.

➔ In the **Save As** dialog box, open the **As** list, choose **Module** then click **OK**.

E. IDE

The IDE (*Integrated Development Environment*) allows you to enter, modify and test your VBA code. IDE is also called the VBA interface or the VBE (*Visual Basic Editor*).

IDE offers a number of features that help you to program and develop your VBA code, such as the object browser, editing assistance and debugging tools.

You can go into the IDE from Access in several ways:

- by pressing the Alt F11 shortcut key,
- by clicking the **Code** ( ) button on the **Database**, the **Form Design** or the **Report Design** toolbar.
- by clicking a module and selecting the **View - Code** menu option,
- by double-clicking a module,
- by selecting an event procedure in a form or report,

– by viewing the **Modules** in the **Database** window and clicking the **New** button or the **Design** button,

IDE windows

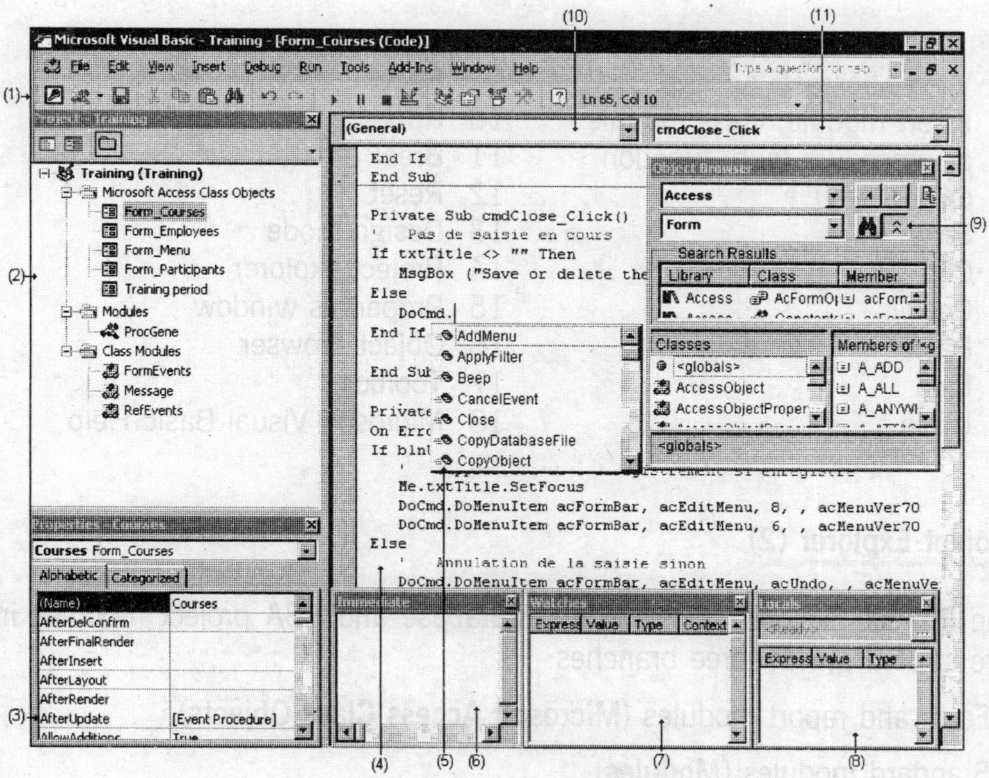

You can access all the IDE windows from the **View** menu.

Standard toolbar (1)

1 View Microsoft Access
2 Insert module, class module or procedure (sub, function or property)
3 Save
4 Cut
5 Copy
6 Paste
7 Find
8 Undo
9 Redo
10 Run
11 Break
12 Reset
13 Design mode
14 Project explorer
15 Properties window
16 Object browser
17 Toolbox
18 Microsoft Visual Basic Help

Project Explorer (2)

The Project Explorer shows all the database and VBA project modules in a tree structure with three branches:

- Form and report modules (**Microsoft Access Class Objects**),
- Standard modules (**Modules**),
- Class modules (**Class Modules**).

Properties Window (3)

The Properties Window displays the properties of the different modules. To view the properties of a form or a report, you must either open the form or report concerned, or select it in the Project Explorer then choose the **View - Object** menu option.

Code Window (4)

The Code Window provides two drop-down list boxes:

- the **Object** box (**10**) lists the module's objects,
- the **Procedure** box (**11**) lists the procedures or the events of the object selected in the **Object** box: events that are already being used appear in bold.

Auto List Members (5)

This drop-down list appears automatically when you enter an object name followed by a dot. It offers the list of methods, properties and constants you can use with this object.

If this list does not appear, select **Tools - Options** and activate the **Auto List Members** option, under the **Editor** tab.

Immediate Window (6)

This window allows you to display and modify variables and to run lines of code.

The **Immediate**, **Locals** and **Watch** windows are used for debugging applications.

Locals Window (7)

This window displays the names and values of all the variables that you can access in the current scope.

Watch Window (8)

This window displays the values of the variables for which you have defined a watch expression.

Object Browser (9)

The Object Browser allows you to view each object's properties, methods and constants.

F. Setting VBA editor options

1. Choosing style settings

By default, VBA keywords, functions and statements appear in **blue**, objects, methods and properties appear in **black**, comments appear in **green** and statements containing errors appear in **red**.

To change the style (color, font and size) of the different code elements, choose the **Tools - Options** menu option and select the **Editor Format** tab.

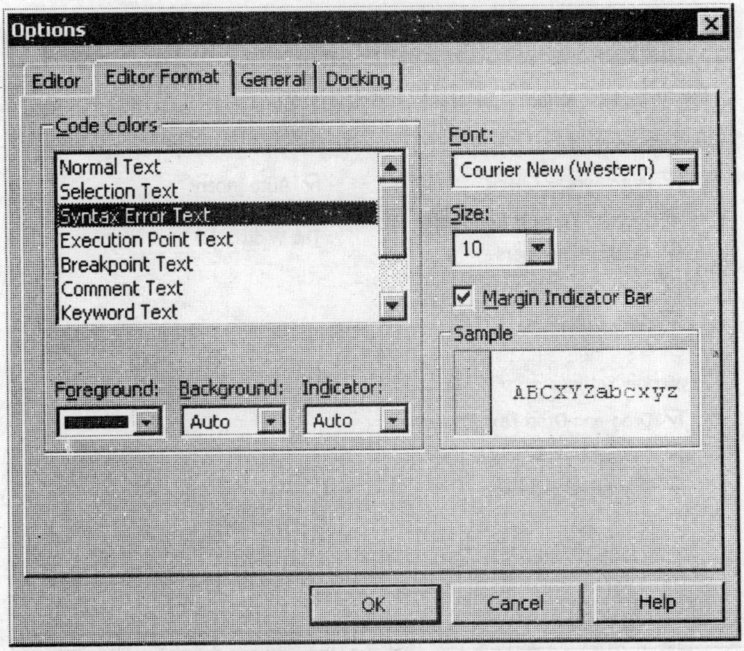

2. Choosing code settings

The VBA editor offers a number of tools that help you to enter and develop your VBA code. These tools include the **Auto Syntax Check**, the **Require Variable Declaration** and the **Auto List Members**.

To activate or deactivate these tools, choose the **Tools - Options** menu option and select the **Editor** tab.

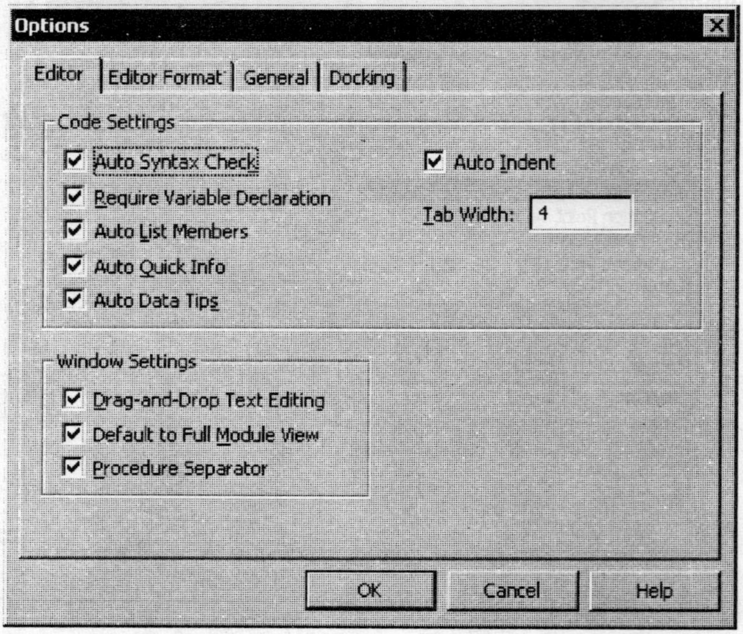

G.Activating object references

To use a data access object, an automation object or a specific ActiveX control, you must activate the reference to the corresponding object library. An object library is generally a .dll or .ocx file that contains object code.

To activate or deactivate a library reference, choose the **Tools - References** menu option.

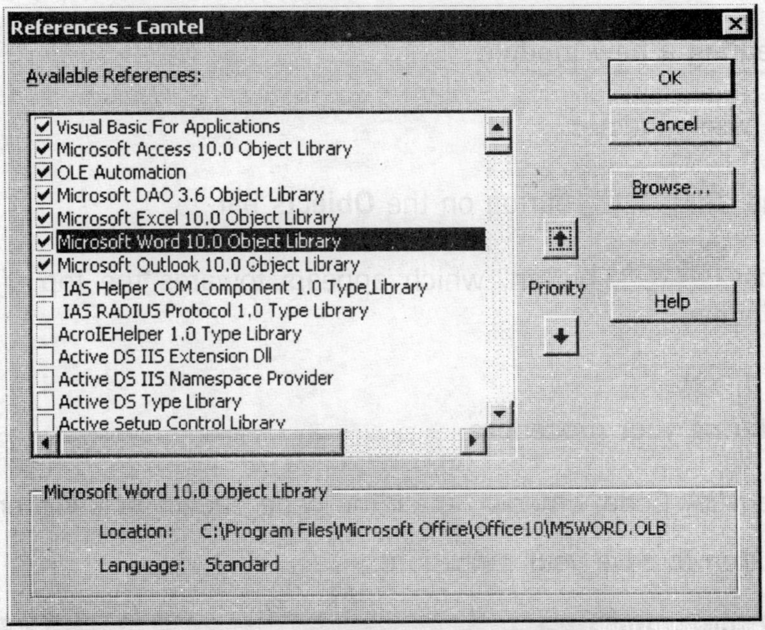

You can add further references to the list of **Available References** using the **Browse** button.

H.Creating a VBA procedure

Here is a step-by-step guide to creating a VBA procedure.

This procedure asks the user to enter a date in abbreviated format (09/09/02, for example). It checks the date and displays it in unabbreviated format (Monday 9 September 2002, for example).

Step 1: creating a new module

In the database window:

- Click the Modules button on the **Objects** bar.
- Click the New button, which appears towards the top of the database window.

Step 2: entering your procedure

Go into the VBA Code window, enter the code shown below then click the tool button to save your procedure.

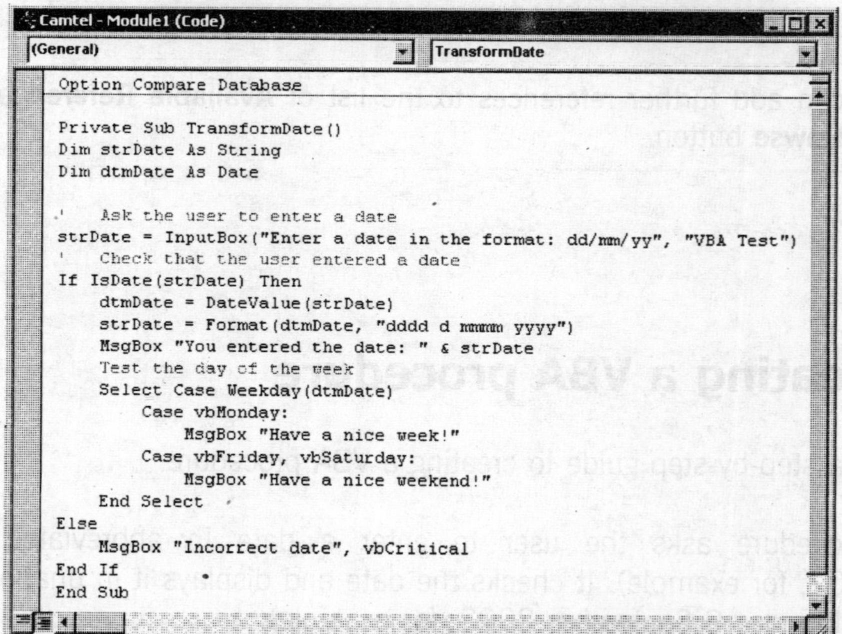

Step 3: testing your procedure

To run the procedure code:

→ Click within the code you entered.

→ Click the ▶ button on the **Standard** toolbar or press the F5 function key.

→ Enter a date in the dialog box that appears and click **OK**.

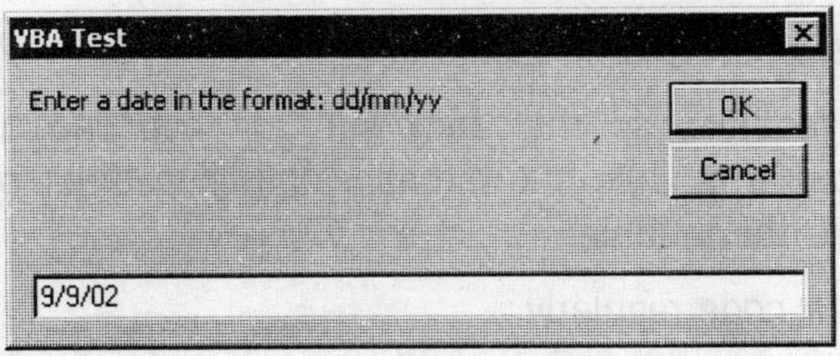

If you entered a valid date, the following message should appear:

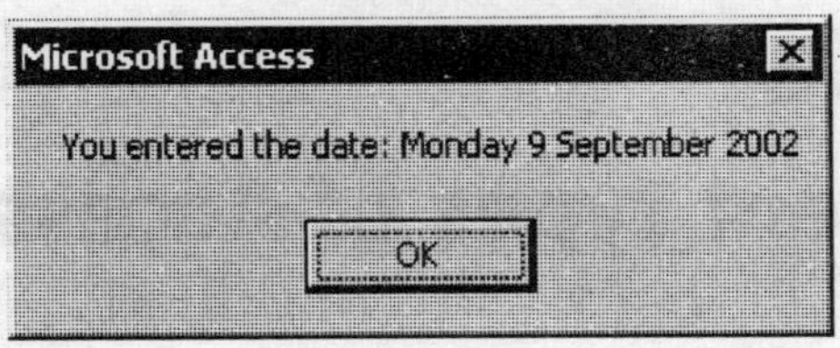

→ Click **OK**.

The following message should appear if you entered a date that falls on a Monday (as in this example):

I. Recommendations

Here are some guidelines to improve the performance of your VBA code:

- Always declare your variables.
- Choose variable types that are as specific as possible.
- Use variables to refer to properties, controls and objects.
- Use the **Me** keyword to refer only to a form or report within an event procedure.
- Use constants wherever you can.
- Design your modules so that they will not overload the memory. The system will load a module into memory, only if another part of the code it is running calls the module.
- Recompile your code regularly.

J. The different types of Access file

Microsoft Access 2002 uses different types of file:

- The .mdb file is the database. This file contains the whole database: the data (the tables), the relationships between the tables (the links), the end-user's interface (forms and reports) and the code (queries, macros and modules).
- The .adp file is the Access project. It allows you to create a client-server application with SQL Server 2000.
- The .mde file contains the database, as does the .mdb file from which it is generated. However, .mde files do not allow users to see its code or modify its forms and reports.

- The .mdw file (system.mdw) is a system database that contains the Access settings and security information on users and groups.
- The .mda file is a libraries database. It can contain code that other different databases can use and code that extends Access' features.
- The .ldb file contains information on locked records in the database. Access manages this file automatically.

Chapter 2: Visual Basic language

A. Modules

Visual Basic distinguishes three types of module:

- standard modules,
- Microsoft Access Class Object modules,
- independent class modules.

The Access **Database** window shows only standard modules.

However, the **Project Explorer** window of the VBA interface lists all the modules in a tree structure:

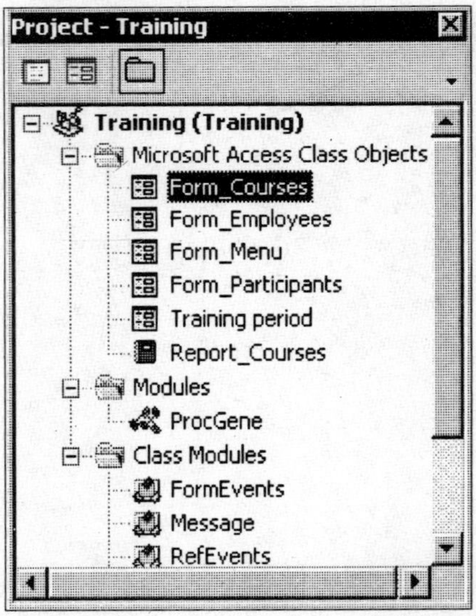

If the **Project Explorer** window is not visible in the VBA interface, select the **View - Project Explorer** menu option or use the Ctrl **R** shortcut key.

The **Microsoft Access Class Object** modules contain event procedures that are associated with forms and reports.

Each of the **standard modules** (listed under **Modules**) contains one or more procedures that you can call in various circumstances from other modules.

It is advisable to group together, in one or more modules, your "utility" procedures that different applications may call (such as date formatting procedures, for example). You will then be able to export these modules to other Access databases using the **Export** option of the **File** menu.

Independent class modules are used to create object classes (Chapter 3, Objects and Collections covers object-oriented programming).

You can use the Visual Basic language elements that this chapter describes in the different types of module.

B. Procedures

Procedures are **subprograms** that you can use to split complex programming tasks into sets of smaller and simpler tasks.

They allow you to organize your code within your modules, to make it easier to maintain and reuse.

Access 2002 VBA distinguishes three types of procedure:

- **Sub** procedures (these are subroutines or subprograms),
- **Function** procedures,
- **Property** procedures.

This chapter describes only the more-frequently used, **Sub** procedures and **Function** procedures. Chapter 3 describes **Property** procedures.

Sub procedures and **Function** procedures have a number of points in common:

- they contain statements and/or VBA methods,
- they accept arguments,
- other **Sub** or **Function** procedures can call them.

The following features are specific to **Function** procedures:

- they can return values,
- you can call them from macros.

1. Sub procedures

There are two types of **Sub** procedure:

- general **Sub** procedures,
- event **Sub** procedures.

A general **Sub** procedure is declared in a standard module or at the general level of a form or report module. Your program code must call such a procedure explicitly.

<u>*Example*</u>

*This general procedure asks the user to confirm his/her wish to leave the application then, if the user replies **Yes**, it leaves Access.*

You can call this code from any command button or menu option that allows the user to leave the application.

```
Private Sub Leave_Appli()
    If MsgBox("Do you want to leave the application?", _
        vbQuestion + vbYesNo) = vbYes Then
        Quit
    End If
End Sub
```

An **event Sub procedure** is associated with an object event: its name is composed of the name of the activated object followed by an underscore character (_) followed by the name of the event. Such a procedure is called implicitly: it will run only when the associated event occurs.

Example

*This event procedure displays the **Employees** form, when the user clicks the **cmdEmployees** command button.*

```
Private Sub cmdEmployees_Click()
    DoCmd.OpenForm "Employees"
End Sub
```

You can generate some event Sub procedures using a wizard (for example, the Command Button Wizard).

2. Function procedures

A **Function procedure**, also called simply a function, returns a value, such as the result of a calculation. The returned value in the function must have the same name as the function.

The Visual Basic language offers a number of integrated functions, such as its date functions (**day**, **week** and **year**, for example).

In addition to these integrated functions, you can create your own custom functions.

Example

*This function asks the user to confirm his/her wish to leave the application. If the user replies **Yes**, it returns **True**. Otherwise it returns **False**.*

```
Function Leave_Appli() As Boolean
    If MsgBox("Do you want to leave the application?", _
        vbQuestion + vbYesNo) = vbYes Then
        Leave_Appli = True
    Else
        Leave_Appli = False
    End If
End Function
```

3. Declaring procedures

Syntax of a Sub procedure

```
[Private | Public | Friend] [Static] Sub
ProcedureName ([argument list])
    <statements>
End Sub
```

Syntax of a Function procedure

```
[Private | Public | Friend] [Static] Function
ProcedureName ([argument list]) [As type]
    <statements>
End Function
```

To create a Sub or Function procedure you must carry out the following steps:

- define the **scope** of the procedure,
- declare the procedure according to its type, with the **Sub** or **Function** keyword followed by the name of the procedure,
- define the **arguments** you want to pass to the procedure (these must appear between brackets immediately after the name of the procedure),
- if you are creating a **Function** procedure, you can (optionally) specify the type of the returned value, following the **As** keyword,
- enter the code that will implement the required processing: you can use **Exit Sub** or **Exit Function** to leave the procedure before reaching the end; if you are creating a **Function** procedure, assign the result to the name of the function,
- close your procedure with **End Sub** or **End Function**.

4. Procedure scope

The scope of a procedure defines its field of application.

You can call a **Public** procedure from any module, from any event procedure or from any macro in the database.

You can call a **Private** procedure only from a procedure within the same module.

You can use a **Friend** procedure only in class modules.

The **Static** keyword indicates that the system must allocate storage space to the procedure's local variables. This means that the local variables will keep their values between calls.

In the absence of the **Public**, **Private** or **Friend** declaration, the procedure is public, by default.

5. Procedure arguments

Arguments allow you to pass data to the procedure. You can use 0, 1 or more arguments.

To declare an argument, you need only specify its name. However, here is the complete syntax of an argument declaration:

```
[Optional] [ByVal | ByRef] [ParamArray]
VariableName [As type]
```

`Optional`	indicates that the argument is optional: all the optional arguments must appear at the end of the argument list and be of the Variant type.
`ByVal`	indicates that the argument is passed by value: the procedure receives a copy of the variable and can not modify the value of the argument source.
`ByRef` (default option)	indicates that the argument is passed by reference: the procedure can access the source variable and can modify its value.
`ParamArray`	is used only as the last argument in the list to indicate that the argument is an optional array of **Variant** type elements: you cannot use this keyword with the **ByVal**, the **ByRef** or the **Optional** keyword.

`VariableName` indicates the name of the argument. In the case of an array variable, you must not indicate the dimensions.

`type` indicates the data type of the argument passed to the procedure (Byte, Boolean, Integer or Long, for example).

6. Named arguments

Passing arguments in a specific order may be inconvenient, especially when some of the arguments are optional. Moreover, using this method to call procedures with several arguments often impairs readability.

→ Named arguments offer the following advantages:

- you do not need to pass the arguments in any specific order,
- you can simply omit any optional arguments.

Here is the syntax of a named argument:

```
ArgumentName := Value
```

Example

```
If MsgBox("Do you want to leave the application?", _
    vbQuestion + vbYesNo, "Sales management") = vbYes Then
    Application.Quit
End If
```

You can transform this code, as follows:

```
If MsgBox(Prompt:="Do you want to leave the application?", _
        Buttons:=vbYesNo + vbQuestion, _
        Title:="Sales management") = vbYes Then
        Application.Quit
End If
```

You can even change the order of the arguments:

```
If MsgBox(Prompt:="Do you want to leave the application?",_
        Title:="Sales management", _
        Buttons:=vbYesNo + vbQuestion) = vbYes Then
        Application.Quit
End If
```

7. Calling a procedure

Syntax

```
[Call] ProcedureName [argument list]
```

If you use the `Call` keyword, the argument list must appear between brackets.

To store the results of a function in a variable, use the following syntax:

```
<variable> = ProcedureName ( [argument list] )
```

8. Procedure examples

When the user clicks the **cmdCalculation** command button in the invoice entry form, this example calculates a discount, as follows:

- 5% discount for invoice amounts equal to or greater than 1000,
- 2% discount for invoice amounts equal to or greater than 200 and less than 1000.
- No discount for invoice amounts less than 200.

Event procedure

```
Private Sub cmdCalculation_Click()
    txtDisAmount = Discount(txtInvAmount)
End Sub
```

This procedure calls the **Discount** function passing the invoice amount as an argument (contained in the **txtInvAmount** text box on the form). The **Discount** function calculates the discount and displays the result directly in the **txtDisAmount** text box on the form.

Function

```
Private Function Discount(Amount As Currency) As Currency
Const Rate1 = 0.05
Const Rate2 = 0.02

    If Amount >= 1000 Then
        Discount = Amount * Rate1
    Else
        If Amount >= 200 Then
            Discount = Amount * Rate2                    .../...
```

```
.../...
        End If
    End If
End Function
```

If the invoice amount is less than 200, **Discount** will keep its initial value of zero.

9. MsgBox function

This integrated function displays a message in a dialog box, along with an optional icon and one, two or three buttons.

Syntax of the MsgBox statement (for a single button)

Use this syntax to display a dialog box with a single button:

```
MsgBox <message> [, [<type>][, <title>]]
```

Syntax of the MsgBox function (for several buttons)

Use this syntax to display a dialog box with several buttons. This function returns a value that tells you which button the user chose.

```
MsgBox(<message> [, <buttons>] [, <title>] [, helpfile, context])
```

`message` This is the prompt text (message) that the dialog box must display.

`buttons`	This is a numeric expression. It is a sum of values that indicates the number and type of buttons, the type of icon, the default button and the modality of the dialog box.
`title`	This is an optional string for display in the title bar of the dialog box.
`helpfile`	This is an optional Help file to provide specific assistance in using the dialog box.
`context`	This is the Help context number.

MsgBox Arguments

Constant	Value	Meaning
	Number and type of buttons	
vbOKOnly	0	Shows **OK** button only (default)
vbOKCancel	1	Shows **OK** and **Cancel** buttons
vbAbortRetryIgnore	2	Shows **Abort**, **Retry**, and **Ignore** buttons
vbYesNoCancel	3	Shows **Yes**, **No**, and **Cancel** buttons
vbYesNo	4	Shows **Yes** and **No** buttons
vbRetryCancel	5	Shows **Retry** and **Cancel** buttons
vbMsgBoxHelpButton	16384	Shows **Help** button in the message box

Constant	Value	Meaning
Type of icon		
vbCritical	16	Shows the **Critical message** icon ().
vbQuestion	32	Shows the Warning query ().
vbExclamation	48	Shows the Warning message ().
vbInformation	64	Shows the information message ().
Button by default		
vbDefaultButton1	0	Defaults to first button.
vbDefaultButton2	256	Defaults to second button.
vbDefaultButton3	512	Defaults to third button.
vbDefaultButton4	768	Defaults to fourth button.
Modality		
vbApplicationModal	0	Shows application modal message box (default): the user must respond to the message that the message box displays before he/she can continue working with the current application.
vbSystemModal	4096	Shows system modal message box: all the applications are paused until the user responds to the message that the message box displays.

Constant	Value	Meaning
VbMsgBoxSet Foreground	65536	Shows the message box window as the foreground windows.
vbMsgBoxRight	524288	Right-aligns text.
vbMsgBoxRtlReading	1048576	Text appears right-to-left for Hebrew and Arabic systems.

Constants also define the return values:

Constant	Value	Meaning
vbOK	1	**OK** button was pressed.
vbCancel	2	**Cancel** button was pressed.
vbAbort	3	**Abort** button was pressed.
vbRetry	4	**Retry** button was pressed.
vbIgnore	5	**Ignore** button was pressed.
vbYes	6	**Yes** button was pressed.
vbNo	7	**No** button was pressed.

Examples using the MsgBox function (with two buttons)

```
Resp = MsgBox("Are you sure you want to do this?", _
292, "Confirmation")
```

or

```
Resp = MsgBox("Are you sure you want to do this?", _
vbYesNo + vbQuestion + vbDefaultButton2, _
"Confirmation")
```

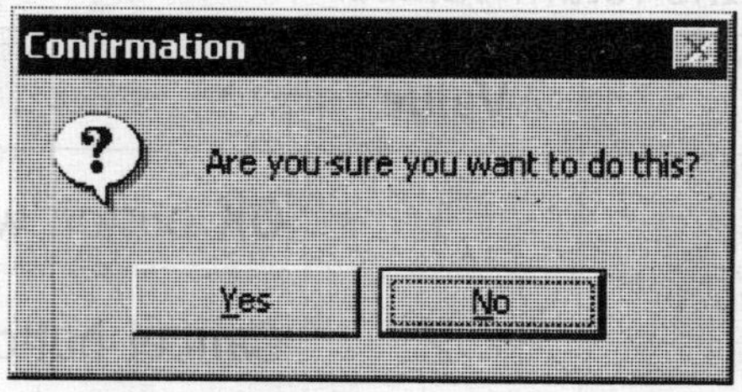

Example using the MsgBox statement (with one button)

```
MsgBox "Incorrect result", vbCritical, "Error"
```

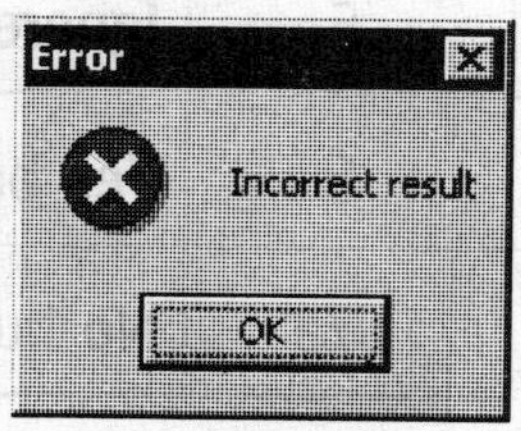

C. Variables

1. Types of variable

Variables allow you to store your working values anywhere in your VBA code and to use them later to make comparisons or to carry out calculations and tests, for example.

You identify a variable by a **name**, which allows you to refer to the value the variable contains and a type, which specifies the sort of data the variable can contain.

Numeric

Type	Scope	Size (bytes)
Byte	0 to 255	1
Integer	-32 768 to 32 767	2
Long	-2 147 483 648 to 2 147 483 647	4
Single (single-precision floating-point)	-3.402823E38 to -1.401298E-45 (for negative values) 1.401298E-45 to 3.402823E38 (for positive values)	4

Type	Scope	Size (bytes)
Double (double-precision floating-point)	-1.79769313486231E308 to 4.94065645841247E-324 (for negative values) 4.94065645841247E-324 to 1.79769313486232E308 (for positive values)	8
Currency (fixed-point)	-922 337 203 685 477.5808 to 922 337 203 685 477.5807	8
Decimal	+/-79 228 162 514 264 337 593 543 950 335 without a decimal separator; +/-7.9228162514264337593543950335 with 28 decimal places to the right of the decimal separator; the smallest non-zero value is +/-0.0000000000000000000000000001	12

Strings

There are two sorts of **String** types:

- variable length strings, which can contain up to approximately 2 billion characters,
- fixed length strings, which can contain from 1 to approximately 64 KB of characters.

Example

```
' Variable length string
Dim Address As String
' Fixed length string (20 characters)
Dim Surname As String * 20
```

Boolean

Boolean variables occupy two bytes and can be either **True** or **False** (the default value).

Date

Date variables occupy eight bytes and can store times and dates from 1 January 100 to 31 December 9999.

Variant

Variant type variables can store all sorts of data, such as dates, floating-point numbers, strings and object references. Variants occupy 16 bytes, plus one byte per character when they store strings.

Object

Object type variables store an object reference in the form of a 4-byte address.
Object is a generic data type. However, to enhance performance, it is preferable to use the name of the object, as defined in the **Classes** pane of the **Object Browser** window.

Example

This example opens an Access database using the generic ***Object*** *type and using the* ***Database*** *object.*

```
Dim dbsEmpl As Object
Dim dbsItem As Database
Set dbsEmpl = OpenDatabase("C\Application\" _
             & "Employees.mdb")
Set dbsItem = OpenDatabase("C\Application\" _
             & "Items.mdb")
```

User-Defined data type

This type is particularly useful for declaring variables that will contain more than one type of data. You can define this type only in the declarations section of a module.

Example

*Declaring a new data type (****Employees****):*

```
Public Type Employees
     Registration_number As String * 5
     Surname As String * 20
     Age As Integer
     Length_of_service As String * 10
End Type
```

*Using the new data type (**Employees**):*

```
Dim NewEmployee As Employees
NewEmployee.Registration_number = "15253"
...
```

2. Declaring variables

You can declare a variable either implicitly or explicitly.

Declaring implicitly

When VBA comes across a variable that was not declared explicitly, it declares it implicitly, giving it a **Variant** type.

Variant types allow you to store values with different data types, successively in the same variable. The variable type changes to suit the value you assign to it.

```
Private Sub Assigning()

' The variable type becomes String:
Var = "Hello"
MsgBox TypeName(Var)

' The variable type becomes Integer:
Var = 12
MsgBox TypeName(Var)
                                        .../...
```

```
.../...
' The variable type becomes Double:
Var = 6.55957
MsgBox TypeName(Var)

' The variable type becomes Boolean:
Var = True
MsgBox TypeName(Var)

End Sub
```

Declaring explicitly

In this case, you must declare your variable before you use it.

You can force explicit declaration of all variables, using the **Option Explicit** statement in the declarations section of each module. To activate this statement by default in VBA, use the **Tools - Options** command and activate the **Require Variable Declaration** option, under the **Editor** tab.

You can declare variables explicitly in the declarations section of the module or in the body of a procedure or a function.

You can declare a variable using a similar syntax, in one of four ways:

- at module level:

```
Private <VariableName> [As type]
Public <VariableName> [As type]
```

- at procedure or function level:

```
Dim <VariableName> [As type]
Static <VariableName> [As type]
```

Each time VBA runs the **Dim** statement, it re-initializes the variable (to 0 for a numeric variable, to an empty string for a **String** variable and to **Empty** for a **Variant** variable). If you want to keep the previous value, you must use **Static** instead of **Dim**.

If you do not specify a type (such as **Dim** or **Var**) VBA assigns the Variant type to the variable.

---

3. Variable scope

A variable is said to be **local** to a function or a procedure if you declare it in the body of the function or the procedure using a **Dim** or a **Static** statement. Such a variable is not visible outside the function or the procedure.

A variable will be visible to all the procedures or functions in the module (standard, class, form or report) if you declare it in the declarations section of the module using a **Private** (or **Dim**) statement.

A variable is said to be **public** to the whole application if you declare it in the declarations section of a module using a **Public** statement. Such a variable is visible from anywhere in the application.

To access a public variable from another form or report module, use the following syntax:

```
Forms!<FormName>.<VariableName>
Reports!<ReportName>.<VariableName>
```

---

4. Arrays

As with other variables, you can declare an array using the **Dim**, **Static**, **Private** or **Public** statement.

Unlike other variables that store only one value at a time, an array can store a set of values.

An array can have up to 60 dimensions.

You can refer to the array globally or you can access individual elements using an index.

Whatever the data type of its elements, an array uses 20 bytes of memory, plus 4 bytes for each dimension plus the number of bytes that the data themselves require.

If you do not specify the data type of your array, VBA assigns the **Variant** type to your array elements.

By default, the index 0 refers to the first element of an array dimension. However, you can set this default value to 1, using the **Option Base 1** statement in the declarations section.

You can define the upper and lower bound of an individual array using the **To** clause in your declaration statement.

Examples

Declaring arrays:

```
' Array with 12 elements, indexed from 0 to 11
Dim Discount(11) As Single
' Array with 12 elements, indexed from 1 to 12
Dim Expenses(1 To 12) As Single
' Array with 2 dimensions:
'    the first indexed from 0 to 10
'    the second indexed from 1 to 15
Dim Grid(10, 1 To 15) As String
```

```
Option Base 1
' Array with 12 elements, indexed from 1 to 12
Dim Expenses(12)
```

Using a two-dimension array.
*The following example creates a multiplication array: each element of the **Multiply** array contains a value equal to the product of its indices:*

```
Dim Multiply(1 To 10, 1 To 10) As Integer
Dim i, j As Integer

' Initializing the array
For i = 1 To 10
    For j = 1 To 10
        Multiply(i, j) = i * j
    Next j
Next i
```

.../...

```
.../...
' Show the result of 4 * 7
MsgBox Multiply(4, 7)
' Show the result of 7 * 4
MsgBox Multiply(7, 4)
```

Dynamic arrays

A dynamic array is an array that you can resize to suit your immediate needs. This technique allows you to use your memory space more efficiently.

Declaring a dynamic array:

```
Dim Dynamic_Array()
```

Using a dynamic array.

Before you use it, you must size your dynamic array using the ***ReDim*** *statement:*

```
ReDim Dynamic_Array(15 To 50)
```

You can use the **ReDim** statement to resize your dynamic array as many times as you like. However, by default VBA will reinitialize your array each time you resize it. To keep the existing values in your array, use the **ReDim Preserve** statement:

```
ReDim Preserve Dynamic_Array(15 To 70)
```

5. Constants

A constant contains a numeric or string value that does not change.

The **Const** statement allows you to declare a constant and to define its value. Once you have declared your constant, you can neither modify it nor assign a new value to it.

You can declare a constant in a procedure or in the declarations section of a module.

Constants declared at module level are **private**, by default.

To declare a public constant at module level, you must use the **Public** keyword at the beginning of your **Const** statement.

Examples

Declaring a constant:

```
Public Const COMPANY = "ENI Publishing"
Const BLACK = &H0&
```

Using a constant:

```
CompanyName = COMPANY
Form!Employees!FirstName.BackColor = BLACK
```

Intrinsic constants

Intrinsic constants are constants that the Microsoft Access 2002 application provides. You can view these constants in the Object Browser.

You can use intrinsic constants in macros or in your VBA code.

The name of each intrinsic constant name bears a two letter prefix. This prefix identifies the objects library that provides the constant.

For example, the names of constants from the Microsoft Access library bear the prefix "ac", while those from the Visual Basic library bear the prefix "vb".

Examples

```
acForm
vbCurrency
```

There are several categories of intrinsic constants (such as action constants or event procedure constants, for example).

D.Control structures

You often need to test specific conditions to decide whether or not to run a sequence of statements.

Control structures allow you to carry out such tests and to choose between different statement sequences. Control structures are also called conditional statements.

VBA provides two basic control structures:

- If ... Then ... Else ...
- Select Case ...

You can also use the **IIf** function to define a value according to a condition.

1. If ... Then ... Else statement

➔ If ... Then ... Else

This statement runs a sequence of statements depending on the value of an expression.

You can nest **If ... Then ... Else** statements as much as you like.

When combined with appropriate indenting, the multi-line syntax of these statements makes them very readable.

One-line syntax

```
If <condition> Then <statements> [Else <statements>]
```

Where <statements> can be one or more statements separated by the colon (:) character.

Block form syntax 1

```
If <condition 1> Then
  <statement sequence 1>
[ElseIf <condition 2> Then
  <statement sequence 2>]
[Else
  <statement sequence 3>]
End If
```

Block form syntax 2

```
If <condition 1> Then
  <statement sequence 1>
[Else
  If <condition 2> Then
   <statement sequence 2>
  [Else
   <statement sequence 3>]
  End If]
End If
```

Example

This example displays the result of comparing A and B:

```
If A > B Then
    MsgBox "A>B"
Else
    If A = B Then
        MsgBox "A=B"
    Else
        MsgBox "A<B"
    End If
End If
```

2. Select Case statement

→ Select Case

This statement runs a sequence of statements depending on the value of an expression.

Although it does a similar job to that of the **If ... Then ... Else** statement, the **Select Case** statement is more readable and more convenient to use when you want to compare the same expression with several different values.

Syntax

```
Select Case <test expression>
   [Case <expression list 1>
     <statement sequence 1>]
   [Case <expression list 2>
     <statement sequence 2>]
   [Case Else
     <statement sequence else>]
End Select
```

Where `<expression list>` can take several forms:

- a value (for example: `Case 10`)
- a list of values (ex: `Case 1, 5, 10`)
- a range of values (for example: `Case 1 To 5`)
- a conditional expression (for example: `Case Is >= 5`)

Example

This example comments on a centigrade temperature:

```
Select Case Temperature
    Case 0
        MsgBox "Freezing"
    Case 1 To 10
        MsgBox "Cold"
    Case 11 To 16                                      .../...
```

```
.../...
        MsgBox "Cool"
    Case 17, 18, 19
        MsgBox "Winter indoor temperature"
    Case 20 To 25
        MsgBox "Pleasant"
    Case Is > 25
        MsgBox "Hot"
    Case Else
        MsgBox "Unclassified temperature"
End Select
```

3. IIf function

➔ IIf

This function returns one of two values, depending on the value of a Boolean expression.

Syntax

```
IIF (<condition>, <value if true>, <value if false>)
```

Example

```
Dim Boo As Boolean
Boo = IIf(A = B, True, False)
```

You can nest several **IIf** functions:

Example

```
Dim Itg As Integer
Itg = IIf(A = B, IIf(B = C, 1, 0), 0)
```

E. Looping structures

Looping (or repeat) structures allow you to repeat the execution of a sequence of statements.

VBA provides several types of looping structure:

```
Do ... Loop

While ... Wend

For ... Next

For Each ... Next
```

Do ... Loop and **While ... Wend** repeat a process until a certain condition is met. On the other hand, **For ... Next** repeats a process the number of times that a counter specifies.

For Each ... Next allows you to run through a number of elements in an array or a collection.

1. Do ... Loop statement

→ Do ... Loop

This statement runs a sequence of statements **While** or **Until** a specified condition is met.

Syntax 1

With this syntax, the statement sequence may not run at all, as it tests the condition before running the sequence.

```
Do [{While | Until} <condition>]
    <statement sequence>
    [Exit Do]
    [<statement sequence>]
Loop
```

Syntax 2

With this syntax, the statement sequence must run at least once, as it tests the condition after running the sequence.

```
Do
    <statement sequence>
    [Exit Do]
    [<statement sequence>]
Loop [{While | Until} <condition>]
```

Exit Do is often used after testing a condition that is internal to the loop. It allows you to leave the loop without testing the loop condition.

Example

*This example displays annual expenses after calculating them from an array (**MonthlyExpenses**) composed of twelve elements that were loaded previously:*

```
Dim IntCtr As Integer
Dim YearsExpenses As Currency

YearsExpenses = 0
IntCtr = 0
Do
    IntCtr = IntCtr + 1
    YearsExpenses = YearsExpenses + MonthlyExpenses(IntCtr)
Loop Until IntCtr = 12

MsgBox "Annual expenses = " & YearsExpenses
```

2. While ... Wend statement

➔ While ... Wend

This statement runs a sequence of statements **While** a specified condition is met.

Syntax

```
While <condition>
    <statement sequence>
Wend
```

Example

*This example displays annual expenses after calculating them from an array (**MonthlyExpenses**) composed of twelve elements that were loaded previously:*

```
Dim IntCtr As Integer
Dim YearsExpenses As Currency

YearsExpenses = 0
IntCtr = 1
While IntCtr <= 12
    YearsExpenses = YearsExpenses + MonthlyExpenses(IntCtr)
    IntCtr = IntCtr + 1
Wend

MsgBox "Annual expenses = " & YearsExpenses
```

3. For ... Next statement

➔ For ... Next

This statement runs a sequence of statements the number of times that a counter specifies.

Syntax

```
For <counter> = <start> To <end> [Step <increment>]
    <statement sequence>
    [Exit For]
    <statement sequence>
Next [<counter> [,<counter2>] [, ...]]
```

Exit For is often used after testing a condition that is internal to the loop. It allows you to leave the loop early.

Example

*This example displays annual expenses after calculating them from an array (**MonthlyExpenses**) composed of twelve elements that were loaded previously:*

```
Dim IntCtr As Integer
Dim YearsExpenses As Currency

YearsExpenses = 0
For IntCtr = 1 To 12
    YearsExpenses = YearsExpenses + MonthlyExpenses(IntCtr)
Next

MsgBox "Annual expenses = " & YearsExpenses
```

The **Step** keyword allows you to increment or decrement the counter variable by a specific amount.

Example

*This example decrements the **j** counter by 5, on each loop. At the end of the loop the **total** variable will contain the sum of 5, 10, 15 and 20.*

```
Dim j As Integer
Dim total As Integer
total = 0
For j = 5 To 20 Step 5
    total = total + j
Next j

MsgBox "The total is " & total
```

4. For Each ... Next statement

➔ For Each ... Next

This statement allows you to run through the elements of an array or a collection.

Syntax

```
For Each <element> In <array>/<collection>
    <statement sequence>
    [Exit For]
    <statement sequence>
Next [<element>]
```

Example

*This example displays the expenses for each month using an array (**MonthlyExpenses**) composed of twelve elements that were loaded previously (Cf. the first **For ... Next** example):*

```
Dim Expenses As Currency

For Each Expenses In MonthlyExpenses
   MsgBox Expenses
Next
```

F. Operators

Operators allow you to carry out arithmetic operations on variables and constants, to compare variables and to test conditions.

There are several categories of operator:

- arithmetic operators,
- comparison operators,
- logical operators,
- string concatenation operator.

The assignment operator is the equal sign (=). The value to the right of the equal sign is assigned to the variable to the left of the equal sign (for example: Int A = 12 or IntA = IntB * 12).

---

1. Arithmetic operators

Arithmetic operators allow you to carry out arithmetic calculations using variables and/or numeric constants.

Operator	Operation
+	Addition
-	Subtraction
/	Division (returning a floating-point result)
Mod	Modulus (returning the remainder of dividing a number by another)
\	Division (returning an integer result)
*	Multiplication
^	Raising a number to power

2. Comparison operators

Comparison operators allow you to compare two numeric values or two string values.

Operator	**Operation**
<	Less than
<=	Less than or equal to
>	Greater than
>=	Greater than or equal to
=	Equal to
<>	Not equal to

When used at module level, the **Option Compare** statement defines the default method for comparing string values. You can define one of three methods:

Option Compare Binary This is the default option, by default. This method compares strings according to a sort order that is based on the internal binary representation of the string characters. For example: A < B < E < Z < a < b < e < z < À < Ê < Ø < à < ê < ø

Option Compare Text This method compares strings according to a case-insensitive sort order. For example: (A=a) < (À=à) < (B=b) < (E=e) < (Ê=ê) < (Z=z) < (Ø=ø)

Option Compare Database	This method compares strings according to a sort order based on the locale ID of the current database.

3. Logical operators

Logical operators allow you to compare two or more Boolean expressions and return a Boolean result. They are generally used with **if** statements.

Operator	**Operation**
And	If all the expressions have True values, this operator returns a True value. If at least one of the expressions has a False value, this operator returns a False value.
Or	If at least one of the expressions has a True value, this operator returns a True value (inclusive-or). Otherwise it returns False.
Xor	If one and only one of the expressions has a True value, this operator returns a True value (exclusive-or). Otherwise it returns False.
Not	This operator returns the logical opposite of the expression value.
Eqv	This operator returns True if two expressions are logically equivalent. Otherwise it returns False.

Examples

(A>=1) And (A<=9) will return True, if **A** is between 1 and 9 inclusive.
Not (A>=10) will return True, if **A** is less than 10.
(A>0) Or (B>0) Or (C>0) will return True, if at least one of these three values is positive.

4. String concatenation operator

The VBA string concatenation operator is the **&** character. This operator concatenates two expressions into a character string.

Example

This example concatenates a first name and a surname with a space between them:

```
StrFullname = Firstname & " " & Surname
```

5. Operator precedence

When an expression contains several operators, Visual Basic evaluates each part of the expression in a predetermined order. This order is called the operator precedence.

VBA evaluates operators in the following order: arithmetic operators followed by comparison operators followed by logical operators. All comparison operators have equal precedence, so Visual Basic evaluates them in the order they appear from left to right.

VBA evaluates arithmetic and logical operators in the following orders of precedence:

Arithmetic operators: ^, *, /, \, Mod, +, -

Logical operators: Not, And, Or, Xor, Eqv

Example

*VBA will evaluate the expression 3 + 4 * 5 as 23: it will first carry out the multiplication (4 * 5) then the addition (+ 3).*

You can override this operator precedence using brackets. VBA will always carry out the operations between brackets before it carries out the others. For example, the expression **(3 + 4) * 5** will produce **35**, as, in this case, VBA will carry out the addition first. To improve the readability of your code, it is advisable to use brackets even when they are not strictly necessary.

G. Writing code

1. Comments

Comments make your programs more readable and easier to maintain.

Syntax

```
Rem <comment>
```
or
```
' <comment>
```

Example

```
'==========================================================
Rem This procedure compares two text fields: txtA and txtB
'==========================================================
Private Sub cmdResult_Click()
  ' if txtA is greater than txtB
    If txtA > txtB Then
        lblResult.Caption = "A>B"
    Else
        ' if txtA equals txtB
        If txtA = txtB Then
            lblResult.Caption = "A=B"
        Else
            ' txtA is less than txtB
            lblResult.Caption = "A<B"
        End If
    End If
End Sub
```

2. Line-continuation character

To write a VBA statement over several lines, use the line-continuation character (_) preceded by a space.

Example

```
If A _
> _
B Then _
```

Of course, written in this way, this code is not very readable, but it shows that you can split your lines up anywhere you want.

3. Indenting

It is important to indent the different levels of your code and to make sure that you align all the statements that are on a given level.
Align your procedure headers and footers on the left and indent the contents of your procedures, one tab to the right.

Indenting makes your code easier to read and understand.

4. Naming procedures, variables and constants

The name of each of your procedures, variables and constants must conform to the following rules:

- it must begin with a letter,
- it must not be longer than 255 characters,
- it can contain letters, numbers and underscores (_),
- it must not contain punctuation characters or spaces,
- it must not be the same as a keyword,
- it must be unique within the same level of scope.

Examples

```
ClientNumber
Client_Number
ClientNumber1
```

H.Naming conventions

It is advisable to use naming conventions for variables, controls and objects. Naming conventions help to standardize your code and to make it more readable and easier to maintain.

1. Variables

It is recommended to use two prefixes in your variable names:

- a first prefix, to indicate the scope of the variable: **g** for global scope, **m** for module scope and no prefix for local scope,
- a second prefix to indicate the type of the variable.

Example

`gstrSurname`	a string type, global variable
`intQuantity`	an integer type, local variable

Type of variable	**Prefix**
Boolean	bln
Byte	byt
Currency	cur
Date, time	dtm
Double	dbl
Error	err
Integer	int
Long	lng
Object	obj
Single	sng
String	str
User-defined	udt
Variant	var

2. Controls

As with variables, you should prefix the names of form and report controls according to their type.

Type of control	**Prefix**
ADO data	ado
Check box	chk
Modifiable list box (combo)	cbo
Command button	cmd
Frame	fra
Option group	grp
Image	img
Label	lbl
Option button	opt
Text box	txt

3. Objects

You should also prefix the names of Access objects and Access object variables.

Type of object	Prefix
Table	tbl
Query	qry
Form	frm
Report	rpt
Macro	mac
Index	idx
Field	fld
Collection	col
Property	pty
Data access page	pag

Chapter 3: Objects and collections

A. Introduction

VBA Access is an object-oriented programming language, even though it does not offer all the features that other languages of this type provide.

Most of the items you can handle in Access are objects: tables, fields, records and forms, for example.

Access organizes its objects in a **tree structure**: some objects contain other objects that contain other objects, etc. For example, The **Application** object contains a number of **Form** objects, each of which contains a number of **Control** objects.

A set of objects of the same type make up a **Collection** (for example the **Forms** collection is the application's set of forms, or **Form** objects).

An object has a set of characteristics that are called its **Properties** (for example a form control will have a size and a color) and a set of actions that are called **Methods** (for example, a **Form** object can have a close method that allows you to close it). The object can respond to **events** that the system or the user provokes (for example, by clicking a command button).

In addition, **Classes** allow you to create objects of the same type. Objects from the same class inherit all the methods, properties and events that are associated with this class. In addition to VBA Access classes, you can create your own classes using class modules.

Access offers several sets of objects:

- general objects (such as form and reports, for example),
- data access objects (DAO model),
- ActiveX data access objects (DAO model).

Each set is organized in a tree structure. This chapter covers the general Microsoft Access objects. The following chapter discusses the data access objects.

B. Access object model

The diagram below describes the relationships between the main global Access objects and collections.

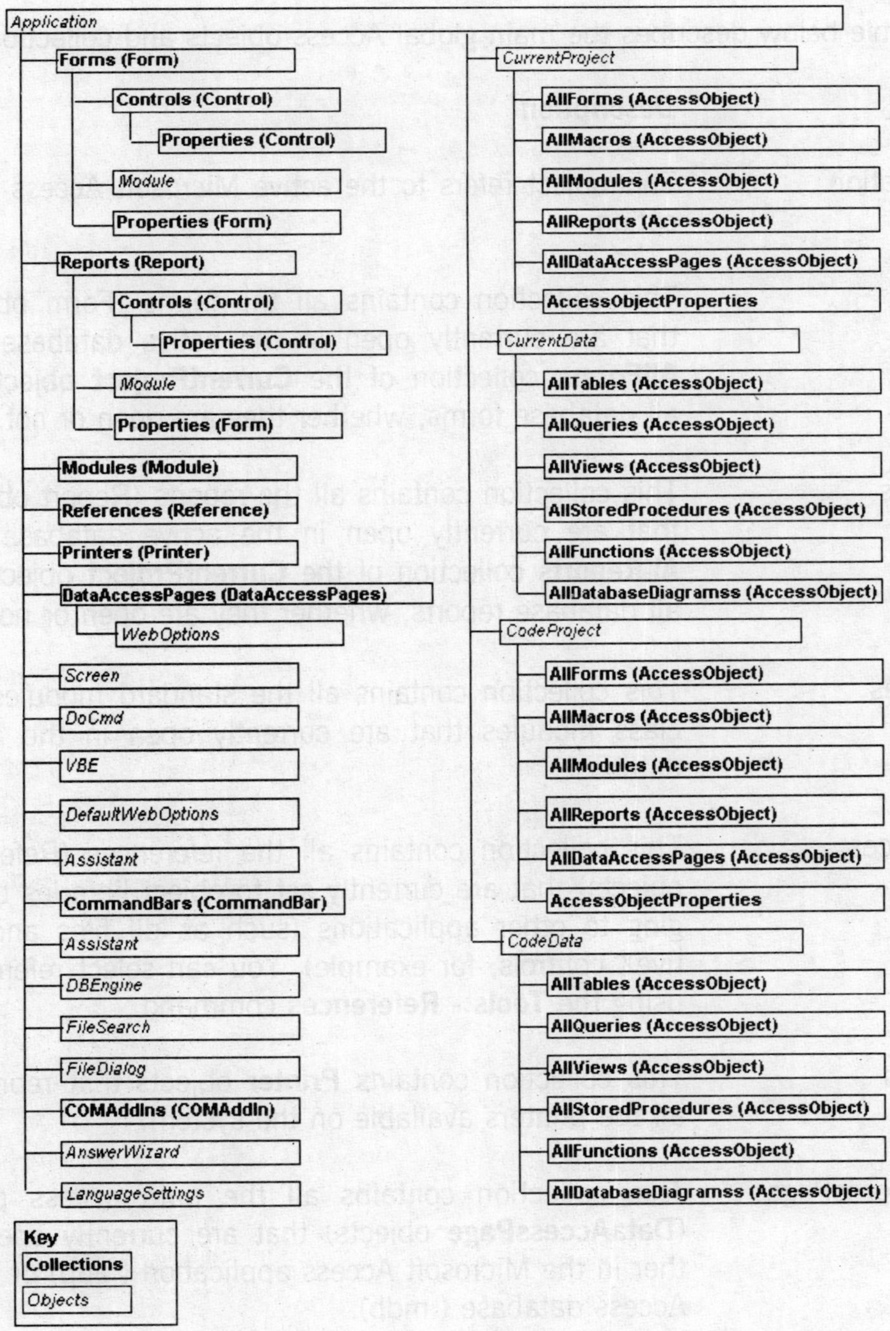
Application
Forms (Form)
Controls (Control)
Properties (Control)
Module
Properties (Form)
Reports (Report)
Controls (Control)
Properties (Control)
Module
Properties (Form)
Modules (Module)
References (Reference)
Printers (Printer)
DataAccessPages (DataAccessPages)
WebOptions
Screen
DoCmd
VBE
DefaultWebOptions
Assistant
CommandBars (CommandBar)
Assistant
DBEngine
FileSearch
FileDialog
COMAddIns (COMAddIn)
AnswerWizard
LanguageSettings
CurrentProject
AllForms (AccessObject)
AllMacros (AccessObject)
AllModules (AccessObject)
AllReports (AccessObject)
AllDataAccessPages (AccessObject)
AccessObjectProperties
CurrentData
AllTables (AccessObject)
AllQueries (AccessObject)
AllViews (AccessObject)
AllStoredProcedures (AccessObject)
AllFunctions (AccessObject)
AllDatabaseDiagramss (AccessObject)
CodeProject
AllForms (AccessObject)
AllMacros (AccessObject)
AllModules (AccessObject)
AllReports (AccessObject)
AllDataAccessPages (AccessObject)
AccessObjectProperties
CodeData
AllTables (AccessObject)
AllQueries (AccessObject)
AllViews (AccessObject)
AllStoredProcedures (AccessObject)
AllFunctions (AccessObject)
AllDatabaseDiagramss (AccessObject)
Key
Collections
Objects

The table below describes the main global Access objects and collections.

Object	**Description**
Application	This object refers to the active Microsoft Access application.
Forms	This collection contains all the forms (Form objects) that are currently open in the active database. The **AllForms** collection of the **CurrentProject** object lists all database forms, whether they are open or not.
Reports	This collection contains all the reports (Report objects) that are currently open in the active database. The **AllReports** collection of the **CurrentProject** object lists all database reports, whether they are open or not.
Modules	This collection contains all the standard modules and class modules that are currently open in the active database.
references	This collection contains all the references (Reference objects) that are currently set to object libraries belonging to other applications (such as dll files and ActiveX controls, for example). You can select references using the **Tools - References** command.
Printers	This collection contains **Printer** objects that represent all the printers available on the system.
DataAccessPages	This collection contains all the data access pages (**DataAccessPage** objects) that are currently open either in the Microsoft Access application (.adp) or in an Access database (.mdb).

Screen	This object provides access to the form, report or control that is currently active.
DoCmd	This object allows you to convert macro actions into Visual Basic. You can convert most macro actions into VBA.
DefaultWebOptions	This object contains the global application-level attributes that Access uses either when you open a Web page or when you save a data access page as a Web page.
Assistant	This object represents the Microsoft Office Assistant. The **Visible** property allows you to display the Assistant and the **On** property allows you to activate the Assistant.
CommandBars	This collection represents the command bars in the active application.
FileSearch	This object allows you to find files in folders.
FileDialog	This object provides access to features similar to those offered by the standard **Open** and **Save** dialog boxes.
COMAddIns	This collection provides information on COM add-ins in the Windows registry.
AnswerWizard	This object represents the Microsoft Office Answer Wizard.
LanguageSettings	This object returns information on the application's language settings.

CurrentProject	This object groups several specific Microsoft Access object collections (for example, the **AllForms** collection of all the database forms).
CurrentData	This object groups several Microsoft Access data access object collections (for example, the **AllTables** collection of all the database tables).

C. Using objects and collections

1. Properties

Properties describe an object. Some properties are read-only properties that VBA code cannot modify.

Syntax

```
{<object> | <object variable>}.<property>
```

Example

```
Dim strVersion As String
' Get the version property of the application object.
' This is a read-only property.
strVersion = Application.Version
' Change the mouse pointer
Screen.MousePointer = 11
```

2. Properties that represent objects

Global objects and objects from classes that VBA provides have properties whose values the system updates automatically.

Property	Object	Contents
ActiveControl	Screen	The active control
ActiveDataAccessPage	Screen	The active page or the page containing the active control
ActiveForm	Screen	The active form
ActiveReport	Screen	The active report
Application	Multiple objects	Access Application object
DBEngine	Application	DBEngine object
Form	Subform control	The form object associated with the Subform control
Me	Form or Report	The Form or Report object whose code is currently running
Module	Form or Report	The module of the Form or Report object
Parent	Multiple objects	The object or collection that contains the object
PreviousControl	Screen	The control object that was previously active

Property	Object	Contents
RecordsetClone	Form	A Recordset clone of the recordset underlying the form
Report	Subreport control	The form object associated with the Subreport control
Section	Form or Report	A section of a form or report

3. Methods

Methods allow you to carry out actions on objects.

Methods are procedures that:

- may use zero or more arguments,
- may or may not return a value (as with **Function** procedures and **Sub** procedures).

Syntax for a method that does not return a value

```
{<object> | <object variable>}.<method> [<Argument list>]
```

Example

```
' Change the Auto Compact option.
' The SetOption method does not return a value.
Application.SetOption "Auto Compact", True
```

You must separate any arguments with commas. If you do not define an optional argument explicitly, the method will use a default value.

Syntax for a method that returns a value

```
<variable> = {<object> | <object variable>}.<method>
([<Argument list>])
```

Example

```
' Boolean variable
Dim blnCompact As Boolean
' Get the Auto Compact option.
' The GetOption method returns a value.
blnCompact = Application.GetOption("Auto Compact")
' Change the Auto Compact option.
' The SetOption method does not return a value.
If Not blnCompact Then
   Application.SetOption "Auto Compact", True
End If
```

4. Events

An event is a **specific action** that has an effect on an object. Microsoft Access objects can respond to several types of event, such as opening and closing forms, clicking the mouse and modifying data, for example. Users provoke most events that occur.

Event procedures allow you to associate code sequences with specific events that take place in a form, a report or a control, etc.

Example

In this example, when the user clicks the "Exit" command button, a dialog box appears to ask the user to confirm his/her action.

```
Private Sub cmdExit_Click()

' Ask the user to confirm
' that he/she wants to leave the application
If MsgBox("Do you want to leave the application?", _
    vbQuestion + vbYesNo) = vbYes Then
  DoCmd.Quit
End If

End Sub
```

As event management is one of the most important fields in the development of an Access application, Chapter 6 of this book is entirely dedicated to this subject.

5. Collections

To refer to an object in a collection, you can use one of the following syntaxes:

```
CollectionName!ObjectName
CollectionName![ObjectName]
CollectionName("ObjectName")
CollectionName(var)
```

where **var** is a string type variable that contains the name of the object.

```
CollectionName(index)
```

where **index** contains the index number of the object in the collection.

To make your code more readable, it is advisable to use the same syntax throughout your application. It is recommended that you use the 3rd and 5th syntaxes as they allow the automatic checking features to act. Moreover, the 5th syntax is very useful to run through the objects of a collection.

For most collections, the first element index is 0. Use indexes only for running through a collection. For example, you should avoid using `Me.controls(5)` to refer to a control, as the control may change if the form is modified.

Example

*This example refers to the **txtStartDate** control of the **Training** form (from the **Forms** and **Controls** collections):*

```
MsgBox Forms("Training").Controls("txtStartDate").Value
' or:
MsgBox Forms!Training.Controls![txtStartDate].Value
```

*This example shows the creation date of a table in the current database (using the **AllTables** collection):*

```
MsgBox CurrentData.AllTables![Training].DateCreated
' or:
MsgBox CurrentData.AllTables("Training").DateCreated
```

This example runs through a collection and changes the font style and color for all the text box controls in the form:

```
Dim Ctl As Control
Dim itg As Integer

For itg = 0 To Me.Controls.Count - 1
    Set Ctl = Me.Controls(itg)
    If TypeOf Ctl Is TextBox Then
        Ctl.ForeColor = vbBlue
        Ctl.FontItalic = True
        Ctl.FontBold = True
    End If
Next itg
```

Default collections

Definition

A default collection is a collection to which you can refer using the name of the object that contains it (without referring to the collection itself).

The following objects have default collections:

Object	Default collection
Container	Documents
Database	TableDefs
DBEngine	Workspaces
Form	Controls

Group	Users
Index	Fields
QueryDef	Parameters
Recordset	Fields
Relation	Fields
Report	Controls
TableDef	Fields
User	Groups
Workspace	Databases

Example

*This example refers to the **txtStartDate** control of the **Training** form (the default collection of a form is the Controls collection).*

```
Forms![Training].[txtStartDate].Value
' or:
Forms!Training.txtStartDate.Value
' or:
Forms!Training!txtStartDate.Value
```

6. Automatic code completion

The VBA editor helps you to use objects. When you type the name of an object that VBA recognizes, followed by a dot, the VBA editor shows a drop-down list of the object's methods and properties. When you select (or type) a method, the VBA editor helps you to enter the different arguments that the method uses.

Example

*Enter the object name **DoCmd** followed by a dot: the following drop-down list appears:*

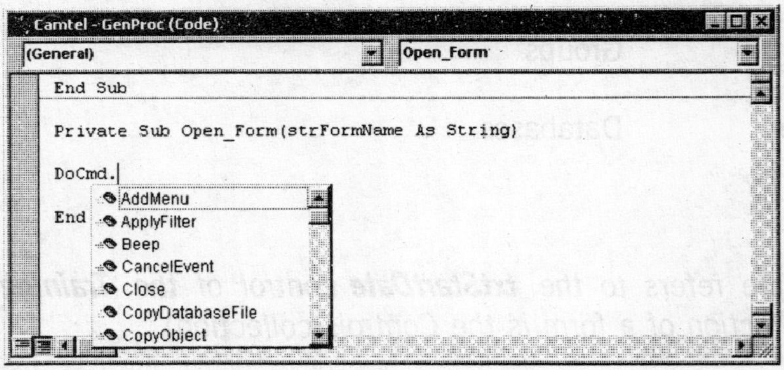

The icon indicates a method and the icon indicates a property.

You can move through the list using the slide bar or by entering the first letters of the method, property or collection that you seek. Double-click a list element to select it.

Type a dot if you have just selected an object and you want to see a list of its properties and methods. If you have just selected a method, type a space to enter the list of its arguments.

*Carrying on with the example, select the **OpenForm** method then type a space:*

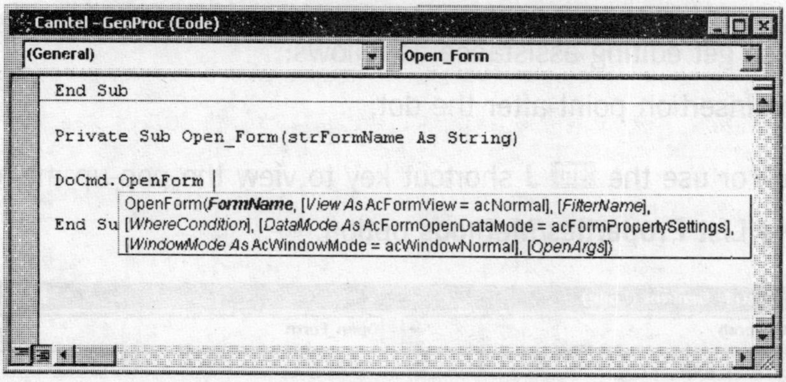

The editor displays a list of the method's arguments and adjusts this list as you continue typing.

Optional arguments appear between square brackets and the current argument appears in bold characters. If there is a set of predefined values for a given argument, a drop-down list of these values appears.

*Carrying on with the example, enter the name of the argument received by the procedure (**strFormName**) followed by three commas (to skip the next two optional arguments):*

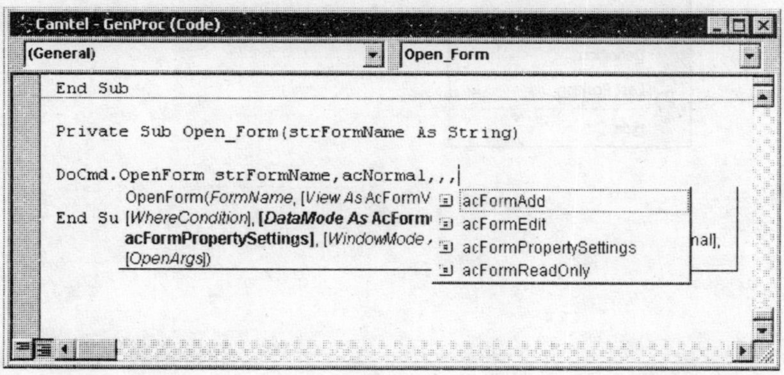

In this example, VBA shows the list of possible values for the **DataMode** argument.

You can also get editing assistance as follows:

- place the insertion point after the dot,
- right-click or use the Ctrl J shortcut key to view the pop-up menu,
- select the **List Properties/Methods** option.

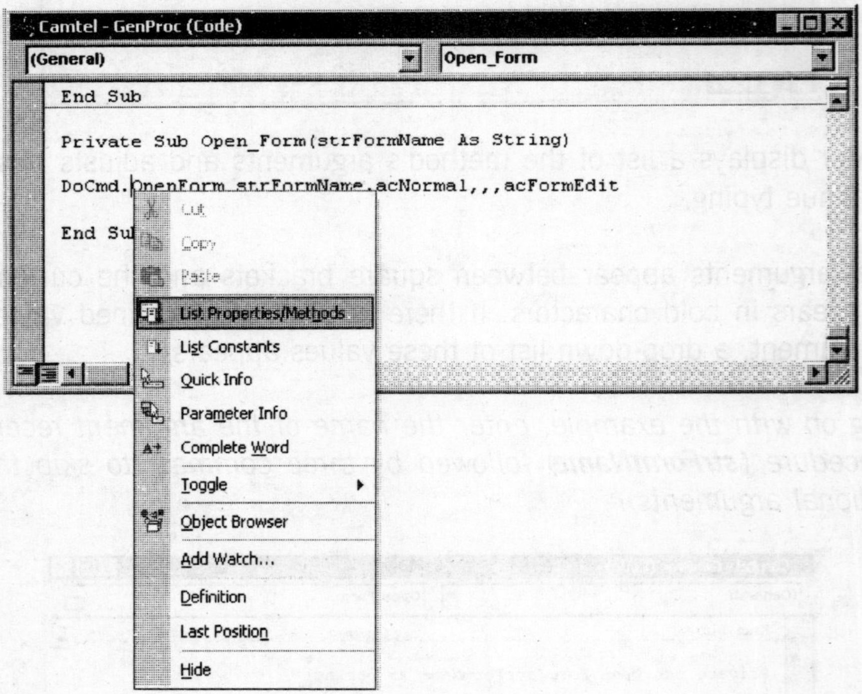

D.Object oriented statements

1. With statement

The **With** statement allows you to carry out a number of operations on an object, after naming it only once.

This approach offers a number of advantages:

- it optimizes the runtime performance,
- it is quicker to program,
- it makes the code more readable.

Syntax

```
With <object>
   <statements using the object's methods and properties>
End With
```

Example

```
' Active object form
With Screen.ActiveForm
    ' Modify the title of the form
    .Caption = "Employee form"
    ' Deactivate the Confirm command button
    .Controls("CmdConfirm").Enabled = False
    ' Go to the 1st control on the 2nd page of the form
    GoToPage 2
End With
```

2. For Each ... Next statement

The **For Each ... Next** statement runs through the objects of a collection or the elements of an array.

Syntax

```
For Each <element> In <array>/<collection>
   <statement sequence>
   [Exit For]
   <statement sequence>
Next [<element>]
```

Example

*This example assigns a font color to each control in the "Employee" form, according to the control's type (using the **ControlType** property). It uses the Form object's default collection, **Screen.ActiveForm**, which is equivalent to **Screen.ActiveForm.Controls**.*

```
Dim ctl As Control
' Run through the controls of the active form
For Each ctl In Screen.ActiveForm
    With ctl
        Select Case ControlType
            ' Labels
            Case acLabel
                .ForeColor = vbBlue
            ' Text boxes
            Case acTextBox
                .ForeColor = vbYellow
            ' List boxes
            Case acListBox, acComboBox
                .ForeColor = vbRed                    .../...
```

```
.../...
        End Select
    End With
Next ctl
```

3. If TypeOf statement

The **If TypeOf** statement tests the type of an object.

Syntax

```
If TypeOf <object> Is <TypeObjet> Then
  <statements using the object's methods and properties>
End If
```

Example

```
If TypeOf ctl Is acListBox Then
    ....
End If
```

4. Set statement

The **Set** statement assigns an object reference to a property or a variable (called an **object variable**).

This statement allows you to assign a reference to an existing object or to create a reference to a new object (possibly using a method to create the object).

Syntax

Creating a reference to a new object

```
Set <ObjectName> = New <ObjectExpression>
```

or

```
Set <ObjectName> = <method that creates the object>
```

`<ObjectName>`	the name of the object variable.
`<ObjectExpression>`	the name of an object or an object variable of the same type.

The **New** keyword creates a new instance of the class. In this case you will lose any reference that the object variable contains.

> To refer to an object using the **New** keyword you must be able to create the object (the ActiveX component must provide a type library; as for the ADO and Excel objects, for example).

Assigning a reference to an existing object

```
Set <ObjectName> = New <ObjectExpression>
```

`<ObjectName>`	the name of the object variable.
`<ObjectExpression>`	the name of an object or object variable of the same type.

Resetting object variables

```
Set <ObjectName> = Nothing
```

The `Nothing` keyword resets the object variable and frees all the system resources and memory that are associated with the object.

Examples

Creating references to new objects:

*Examples 1 and 2 create a new table and add it to the current database. To run these examples, you must have selected the **Microsoft DAO 3.6 Object Library** reference for the project (using the **Tools - References** command).*

Example 1: using the New keyword

```
Dim tdfClient As DAO.TableDef
Dim fld As DAO.Field

' Define the table
Set tdfClient = New DAO.TableDef
tdfClient.Name = "Clients"
' Create the 1st field
Set fld = New DAO.Field
With fld
    .Name = "Cli_Name"
    .Type = dbText
    .Size = 40
End With

tdfClient.Fields.Append fld
' Create the 2nd field
Set fld = New DAO.Field
With fld
    .Name = "Cli_Workforce"
    .Type = dbInteger
End With
```

.../...

```
.../...
tdfClient.Fields.Append fld
' Add the table to the current database
Application.CurrentDb.TableDefs.Append tdfClient

' Reset the object variables
Set tdfClient = Nothing
Set fld = Nothing
```

Example 2: does the same job as Example 1, using methods

```
Dim tdfClient As DAO.TableDef
Dim fld As DAO.Field

' Define the table
Set tdfClient = CurrentDb.CreateTableDef("Clients")
With tdfClient
    ' Create the 1st field
    Set fld = .CreateField("Cli_Name", dbText, 40)
    .Fields.Append fld
    ' Create the 2nd field (2nd method)
    .Fields.Append .CreateField("Cli_Workforce", dbInteger)
End With
' Add the table to the current database
CurrentDb.TableDefs.Append tdfClient

' Reset the object variables
Set fld = Nothing
Set tdfClient = Nothing
```

Example 3

This example creates a form with a text box and a label.

```
' Form object
Dim frmEmployee As Form
' Name of the form
Dim strName As String
' Control object
Dim ctl As Control

' Create a new form
Set frmEmployee = Application.CreateForm
With frmEmployee
    ' Define the title of the form
    .Caption = "Employees"
    ' Set width and height of the form
    .Width = 5000
    .Section(acDetail).Height = 2000
    ' Remove navigation buttons
    .NavigationButtons = False
    ' Remove record selectors
    .RecordSelectors = False
    ' Center the form in the application
    .AutoCenter = True
    ' Define the name of the form
    strName = frmEmployee.Name
End With

' Add the employee name text box
Set ctl = Application.CreateControl(strName, _
        acTextBox, , "", "", 2000, 500, 2500, 300)            .../...
```

```
.../...
' Format the text box
With ctl
    ' Define the name of the text box
    .Name = "lblName"
    ' Set the colors
    .BackColor = vbWhite
    .ForeColor = vbBlack
    .FontBold = True
End With

' Add the employee name label
Set ctl = Application.CreateControl(strName, _
          acLabel, , "", "", 500, 500, 1500, 300)
' Format the label
With ctl
    ' Define the name of the label
    .Name = "lblName"
    ' Define the title of the label
    .Caption = "Name of the employee: "
    ' Set the colors
    .BackColor = vbWhite
    .ForeColor = vbBlue
End With

' Save the form
DoCmd.Save , "Employees"
DoCmd.Close
```

Creating references to existing objects

This example changes the color of a control in a form.

```
' Form object
Dim frm As Form
' Control object
Dim ctl As Control
' Open the Employees form
DoCmd.OpenForm "Employees"
' Assign a variable to the frm object
Set frm = Screen.ActiveForm
' Assign a variable to the ctl object
Set ctl = frm("lblName")
With ctl
     .ForeColor = vbRed
End With
```

E. Object classes

1. Introduction

A **class** acts as a sort of mold that allows you to create objects. For example, suppose you use a mold to create ornamental figures: these figures can then have different colors and clothing. Similarly, you can use a **Class** to create **Objects** to which you can apply different colors and formats.

Objects from the same class will inherit the class' methods, properties and events. Subsequently, you can adapt the characteristics and actions of each of these objects to meet the needs of your application.

In fact, every Access object comes from a class.

2. Class modules

Class modules allow you to create and handle your own object types in your applications.

Class modules have the following characteristics:

- they bear the same name as the object,
- they have public **Sub** and **Function** procedures that define the object's methods,
- they have **Property Get** procedures that allow you to read the object's property values and **Property Set/Property Let** procedures that allow you to define the values of these properties.

When you have written all these procedures in a class module, you can create a new object of the defined type. For this purpose, you can create a new instance of this class using an object variable of the class' type:

```
Dim <ObjectName> As New <ClassName>
```

In fact, class modules are not very common in VBA code as only advanced developers tend to use them.

3. Class module example

This example provides a step-by-step guide to creating and using a class module. This module allows you to display user messages.

This module has the following items:

- One **Confirmation** method: this method displays a dialog box that asks the user to answer **Yes** or **No** to a question and receives the response from the user,
- Two properties: the **IsBeep** property indicates whether or not a beep sound must be omitted before the message is displayed; the **Title** property contains the title of the dialog box.

Example:

To create a module, select the **Insert - Class Module** menu option.

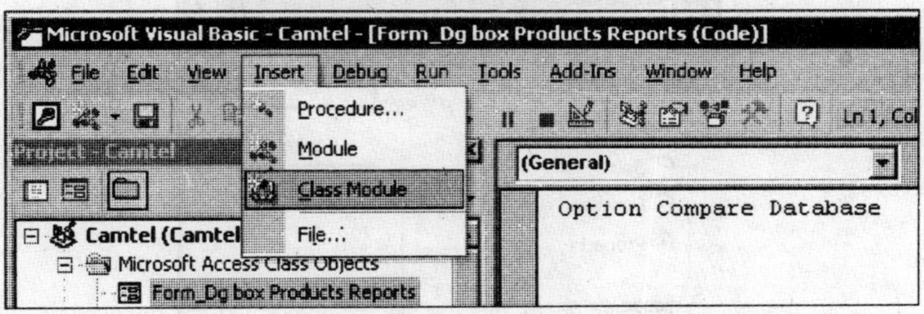

Next, enter the **Name** of the class module (**Message** in this example).

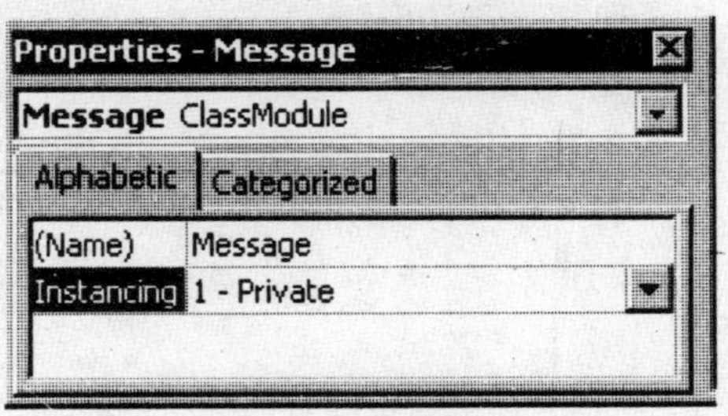

If the **Properties** window is not visible, choose the **View - Properties Window** menu option or press the F4 key.

Define the variables that you will need, to use the properties in the **Message** class module. This code associates the **strTitle** variable with the **Title** property and the **blnBeep** variable with the **IsBeep** property:

```
Option Compare Database
Option Explicit
' Emit a sound
Dim blnBeep As Boolean
' Title of the MsgBox window
Dim strTitle As String
```

Use the **Insert - Procedure** menu option to create the **IsBeep** and **Title** properties.

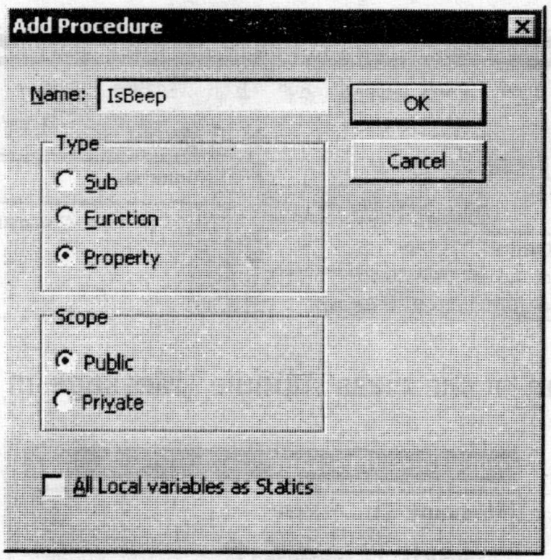

*This action creates the **Property Get** procedure and the **Property Let** procedure for each property. Modify these procedures to obtain the following code:*

```
Public Property Get IsBeep() As Boolean
    IsBeep = blnBeep
End Property

Public Property Let IsBeep(ByVal blnNewValue As Boolean)
    blnBeep = blnNewValue
End Property

Public Property Get Title() As String
    Title = strTitle
End Property

Public Property Let Title(ByVal strNewValue As String)
    strTitle = strNewValue
End Property
```

Use the **Insert - Procedure** menu option to create the **Confirmation** method.

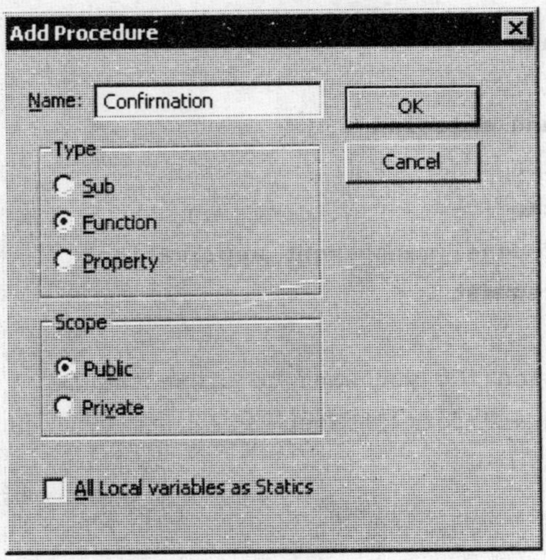

Modify the **Confirmation** procedure to obtain the following code:

```
Public Function Confirmation(strMsg) As Boolean
    If MsgBox(strMsg, vbYesNo, strTitle) = vbYes Then
        Confirmation = True
    Else
        Confirmation = False
    End If
    If blnBeep Then Beep
End Function
```

This method uses the two variables: **strTitle** and **blnBeep**. The method was created as a function, as it must return the user's response (in the form of a Boolean variable).

Once you have created this class, you can use it in a form. For this purpose, create the **Employees** form with two command buttons: **cmdClose** and **cmdExit**. Assign the following code to **click** events:

```
Private Sub CmdClose_Click()
' Message object
Dim msg As New Message

    ' Deactivate sound emission
    msg.IsBeep = False
    ' Dialog box title
    msg.Title = "Personnel management application"
    ' Confirmation request

    If msg.Confirmation("Do you want to close the " _
        & Me.Caption & " form?") Then
        DoCmd.Close
    End If
End Sub                                                   .../...
```

```
.../...
Private Sub CmdQuit_Click()

' Message object
Dim msg As New Message

    ' Activate sound emission
    msg.IsBeep = True
    ' Dialog box title
    msg.Title = "Personnel management application"
    ' Confirmation request
    If msg.Confirmation("Leave the application?") Then
        DoCmd.Quit
    End If

End Sub
```

Next, test your form. The dialog box that the **Confirmation** method displays uses the two properties and returns the user's response.

You can enhance your **Message** class module by defining new properties and methods (to display error messages, for example).

F. Object browser

1. Introduction

With the large and varied range of objects that Access provides, it is important to be able to access object information rapidly.

The Object Browser displays information on objects, methods, properties, events and constants.

You can access the Object Browser in different ways:

- choose the **View - Object Browser** menu option,
- press the F2 key,
- click the tool button.

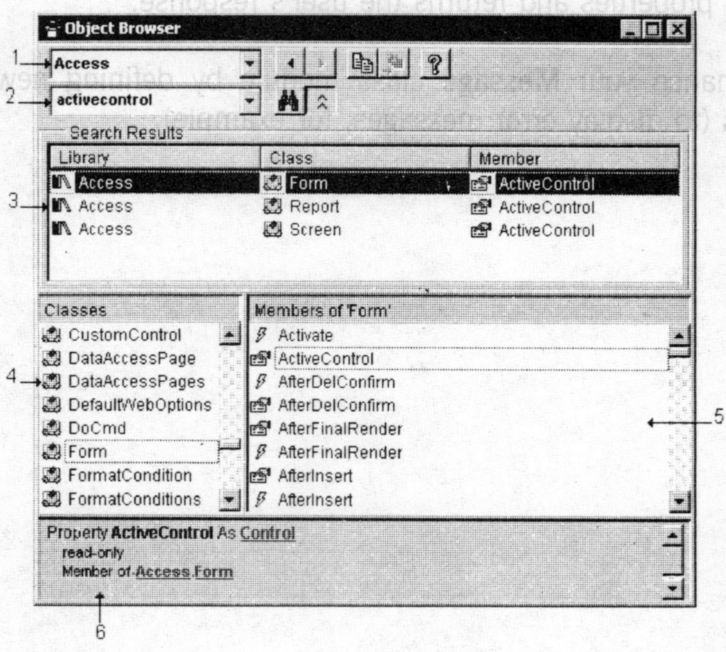

1. lists the object libraries that are currently loaded.

2. shows the search text (defining an object, a property, a collection, an event, a method, etc.).

3. shows the results of the search: as a list of object classes (for objects and collections) and the members they contain (for objects, collections, properties, events or methods).

4. shows the library objects: the selected object class appears in a dotted border.

5. shows the methods, properties, events and constants of the object selected or bordered in the left-hand list. The member selected in the **Search Results** list appears in a border.

6. shows details of the selected item.

The **Message** class created previously appears amongst the library objects with its properties and methods.

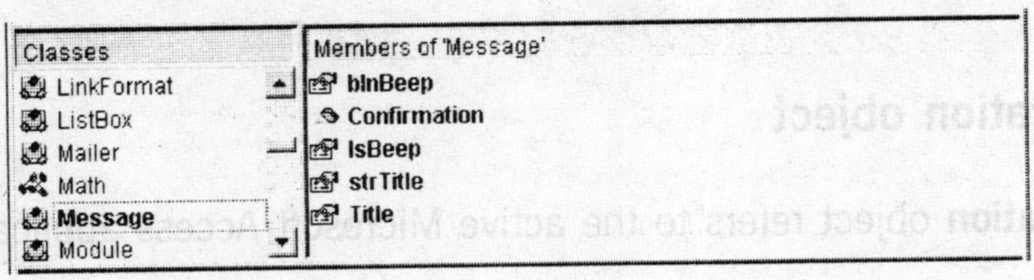

2. Searching the Object Browser

You can search the Object Browser as follows:

– enter your search text in the second list box of the **Object Browser** dialog box,

- click the  icon,
- If the **Search Results** pane shows more than one line, move up or down in the list, as necessary: the **Class** and **Members** panes update automatically.

G. Properties and methods of Access objects

This section describes the properties and methods of commonly used Access objects. Chapter 8 describes the **Form** and **Report** objects.

For an exhaustive list of objects with their properties and methods, look in the VBA help application or use the Object Browser.

1. Application object

The **Application** object refers to the active Microsoft Access application.

Properties

CodeContextObject returns the name of the object in which a macro or Visual Basic code is currently running.

CodeObjectName returns the name of the active database object (table, query, form, report, macro or module).

CurrentObjectType	returns the type of the active database object.
FeatureInstall	specifies or determines how Microsoft Access manages method and property calls that need features you have not yet installed.
IsCompiled	returns a Boolean value that indicates whether or not the Visual Basic project has been compiled.
MenuBar	determines the menu bar to use for the database.
Name	returns the name of the object.
Parent	returns the name of the parent object.
ProductCode	returns the GUID (Globally Unique IDentifier).
ShortcutMenuBar	specifies the shortcut menu that will appear when the user right-clicks.
UserControl	determines whether the active Microsoft Access application was started by the user or by another application using automation technology.
Visible	hides or displays the application.

Methods

AccessError	returns the text string for a Microsoft Access error or a DAO error.
AddToFavorites	adds a hyperlink address to the **Favorites** folder.

BuildCriteria	helps you to build filter criteria.
CloseCurrentDatabase	closes the current database from another application that has opened a database using Automation.
DefaultWorkspaceClone	creates a new Workspace object without the user having to log on again.
Echo	specifies whether or not Microsoft Access must repaint the screen.
FollowHyperLink	opens the document or Web page to which a hyperlink points.
GetOption	returns the current value of an option in the **Options** dialog box.
NewCurrentDatabase	creates a new database in the Microsoft Access window.
OpenCurrentDatabase	opens an existing database as the current database.
Quit	quits Microsoft Access.
RefreshDatabaseWindow	refreshes the **Database** window when a table, a query, a form, a report, a macro or a module has been created, deleted or renamed.
RefreshTitleBar	refreshes the Microsoft Access title bar.
Run	runs a Microsoft or user-defined Function or Sub procedure.

RunCommand runs a built-in menu or toolbar command.

SetOption defines the current value of an option in the **Options** dialog box.

Example

This example defines a command button to save all the objects and leave Access.

```
Sub cmdQuit_Click()
    Application.Quit acSaveYes
End Sub
```

Example

*This example changes the default datasheet colors (you can access these colors under the **Datasheet** tab of the Microsoft Access **Options** dialog box).*

```
' Set default font color to dark blue
Application.SetOption "Default Font Color", 4
' Set default background color to white
Application.SetOption "Default Background Color", 15
' Set default gridlines color to blue
Application.SetOption "Default Gridlines Color", 12
```

2. DoCmd object

The **DoCmd** object allows you to run, in Visual Basic, most of the actions you can run with macros.

A method corresponds to each macro action and the action's arguments become the method's arguments. The **DoCmd** object has no properties.

Here are the **DoCmd** methods:

Running general actions

CancelEvent	cancels an event.
OpenQuery	opens a query.
Quit	leaves Access.
RunCommand	runs a menu or toolbar command.
RunMacro	runs a macro.
RunSql	runs an SQL statement.

Handling form and report data

ApplyFilter	applies a filter to a table, a form or a report.
FindNext	finds the next search item.
FindRecord	finds a record.
GotoControl	moves the focus to a control.
GotoPage	moves the focus to the first control on the specified page or the active form.
GotoRecord	goes to a record.

Importing/exporting data

OutputTo exports an Access object (a table or a form) to another Access database or to another type of file (such as an Excel or an XML file, for example).

SendObject exports an object to an e-mail application.

TransferDatabase imports or exports a database.

TransferSpreadSheet imports or exports a spreadsheet.

TransferText imports or exports ASCII text.

Handling objects

Close closes an object (such as a form or a report).

CopyObject copies an Access object to the same database or to another database.

DeleteObject deletes an object.

Maximize enlarges a window.

Minimize reduces a window.

MoveSize moves or resizes a window.

OpenForm opens a form.

OpenModule opens a VBA module

OpenQuery opens a query.

OpenReport opens a report.

OpenTable opens a table.

OpenView opens an Access view.

PrintOut prints an object.

Rename renames an object.

RepaintObject repaints an object (such as a form, for example).

Requery updates the data on the screen (reruns the object source query).

Restore restores a window to its previous size.

Save saves the active or specified object.

SelectObject selects a database object.

ShowAllRecords deactivates a filter and redisplays all the records.

Miscellaneous

AddMenu creates a menu bar or a shortcut menu.

Beep emits a beep sound.

Echo hides or shows the results of an action as it runs.

Hourglass sets the mouse pointer as an hourglass icon.

SetMenuItem sets or resets global or custom menu items for the active window.

SetWarnings activates or deactivates the display of standard warning messages.

ShowToolbar shows or hides a toolbar.

Macro actions that the DoCmd object does not support

MsgBox Use the **MsgBox** function.

RunApp Use the **Shell** function.

RunCode Call the function directly from your VBA code.

SendKeys Use the **SendKeys** statement.

Visual Basic does not offer equivalents to the **StopAllMacros** and the **StopMacro** macro actions.

3. Screen object

The **Screen** object refers to the active object, whether it is a form, a data access page, a report or a control.

The **Screen** object is mainly used by the event procedures of these objects. The **Screen** object has no methods, only properties:

Properties

ActiveControl	refers to the active control.
ActiveDataAccessPage	refers to the active data access page.
ActiveDataSheet	refers to the active datasheet.
ActiveForm	refers to the active form.
ActiveReport	refers to the active report.
Application	provides access to the Application object and its properties.
MousePointer	specifies the type of mouse pointer.
Parent	refers to the parent object of a control, a section or a subform, etc.
PreviousControl	refers to the control that last received the focus, before the active control.

Example

```
' Show the name of the previous control
Dim ctl As Control
Set ctl = Screen.PreviousControl
MsgBox ctl.Name

' Set the mouse pointer as an hourglass
Screen.MousePointer = 11

' Restore the default pointer
Screen.MousePointer = 0

' Show the name of the active form
Dim frm As Form
Set frm = Screen.ActiveForm
MsgBox frm.Name

' Change the title of the form
frm.Caption = "Employee entry form"
```

4. FileSearch object

This object allows you to search for files according to a set of criteria and to get information on these files.

Properties

General properties:

Creator	returns the four-character code of the application in which the specified object was created (only the Macintosh environment supports this property).
FileName	returns or defines the name of the file you want to find.
FileType	returns or defines the type of the file you want to find.
LastModified	returns or defines a constant that indicates the amount of time since the file was last modified.
LookIn	returns or defines the folder you want to search.
MatchTextExactly	indicates whether or not to search only for files whose text or properties contain the exact word or phrase you specify.
SearchSubFolders	indicates whether or not to search the subfolders of the specified folder.
TextOrProperty	returns or defines the word or the phrase to be sought in the files' text or properties.

Properties returning collections:

FoundFiles	returns the **FoundFiles** object collection that represents the files found by the search.
PropertyTests	returns the **PropertyTests** object collection that represents the set of search criteria for a file search.

SearchFolders returns the **SearchFolders** object collection that represents the set of folders you want to search.

Methods

Execute runs the search for the specified file(s).

NewSearch restores the default search criteria.

RefreshScopes refreshes the list of the **ScopeFolder** objects that are currently available.

Example

*This example stores, in an array, the list of Excel files that the **My Documents** folder contains.*

```
Dim strFileName() As String
Dim i, j As Integer
With Application.FileSearch
    .NewSearch
    .LookIn = "C:\My Documents"
    .SearchSubFolders = True
    .Filename = "xls"
    .MatchTextExactly = True
    .Execute
    j = .FoundFiles.Count
    ReDim strFileName(j)
    For i = 1 To j
        strFileName(i) = .FoundFiles(i)
    Next i
End With
```

5. References collection

The **References** collection contains **Reference** objects that correspond to object libraries from other applications.

To add (or remove) a reference to an object library, choose the **Tools - References** menu option. The following dialog box allows you to select the references you require:

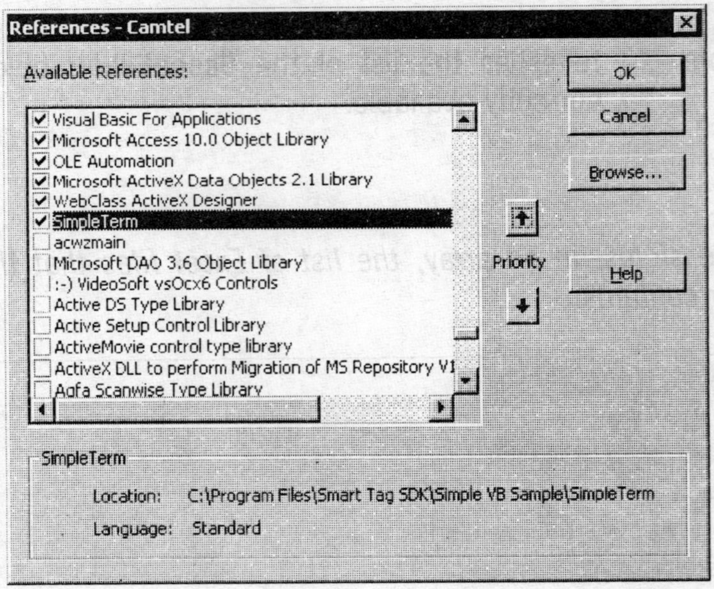

Properties of the References collection

Count returns the number of References objects.

Parent refers to the parent object.

Methods

AddFromFile	creates a reference to a library, from a file name.
AddFromGuid	creates a reference to a library, from its GUID (Globally Unique IDentifier).
Item	returns a collection member according to its position or to a key.
Remove	deletes a member of the **References** collection.

Properties of the Reference object

BuiltIn	indicates whether or not a Reference object points to a default reference that Access needs to run properly.
FullPath	returns the access path and file name of the referenced library.
Guid	returns the GUID, which identifies the library in the Windows registry.
IsBroken	indicates whether or not the object points to a valid reference in the Windows Registry.
Kind	returns the reference type.
Major	indicates the major version number of an application for which you have an associated reference.
Minor	indicates the minor version number of an application for which you have an associated reference.

Name specifies or returns the name of the object.

```
Dim ref As Reference

' Show the total number of references
MsgBox "The total number of references is: " & References.Count
' Show the name and access path of each reference
For Each ref In Application.References
    MsgBox " Name: " & ref.Name & " " & vbCr & vbCr _
    & " Path: " & ref.FullPath
    ' Delete references that are not obligatory for Access
    If Not ref.BuiltIn Then
        References.Remove ref
    End If
Next ref

' Add the Excel objects library
Application.References.AddFromFile "Excel9.olb"
' Add the Word objects library
Application.References.AddFromFile "MsWord.olb"
```

6. Printers collection

The **Printers** collection contains **Printer** objects that represent the printers that are currently available on the system.

Previous versions of Access did not offer the **Printer** object.

Properties of the Printer object

BottomMargin specifies the bottom margin of the page (this object also offers the **TopMargin**, **RightMargin** and **LeftMargin** properties).

ColorMode specifies or returns whether the printer must print in color (**acPRCMColor**) or not (**acPRCMMonochrome**).

ColumnSpacing specifies or returns the vertical spacing between detail sections in a form.

Copies specifies the number of copies to print.

DataOnly allows you to print only the data from a table or a query in datasheet mode.

DeviceName indicates the name of the printer device.

DriverName indicates the driver that the printer uses.

Duplex indicates how the printer manages duplex printing.

Orientation indicates the print orientation (**acPRORPortrait** or **acPRORLandscape**).

PaperBin indicates the paper tray the printer must use.

PaperSize indicates the size of paper the printer must use.

Port indicates the port used for the printer.

PrintQuality indicates the resolution the printer must use.

The other properties (such as **ColumnSpacing**, **RowSpacing** and **ItemSize-Height**) allow you to format the **Detail** section of a form or a report.

Chapter 4: Data access objects

A. DAO and ADO data access tools

VBA data access objects are very useful: you can use them to handle data (to carry out searches, update values, add records and so forth) in **local** or **remote** databases.

Pre-2000 versions of Access offered only the **DAO (Data Access Objects) model**.

Access 2000 provided the **ADO (ActiveX Data Objects)** as well.

Microsoft recommends the ADO model for the following reasons:

- it provides better support for SQL Server,
- it offers better performance in a client/server environment,
- it makes your VBA code shorter and simpler.

You can use the ADO model to develop **a new application** even if your application accesses a local Access database. If you then migrate your data using SQL Server 2000 Desktop Engine or MSDE (MicroSoft Data Engine), your code will run optimally.

If you want to upgrade **an existing application** that uses the DAO model, you can modify your code by transforming your DAO objects to ADO objects.

B. DAO data access model

1. Introduction

The DAO (*Data Access Objects*) object library supports two different database environments, known as workspaces:

- **Microsoft Jet workspaces**: provide access to Access databases and to ODBC (*Open Database Connectivity*) database servers. You can also use them to access external databases such as dBASE, Microsoft Excel and Paradox via an ISAM (*Indexed Sequential Access Method*) driver.
- **ODBCDirect workspaces**: allow you to access ODBC database servers "directly", without loading the Microsoft Jet database engine. This feature makes these workspaces very suitable for running queries, stored procedures or ODBC-specific functions on a remote SQL Server.

To use the DAO object library, you must tick the **Microsoft DAO 3.6 Object Library** reference in the object library reference list (to access this list, select the **Tools - References** menu option in the VBA window).

If this reference is not available in this list, you must select the DAO360.dll file, using the **Browse** button. This file generally resides in the folder C:\Program Files\Common Files\Microsoft Shared\DAO.

In the same folder the DAO360.chm Help file provides detailed explanations on using the DAO model.

2. DAO object model

Microsoft Data Access Objects (DAO) 3.6 object model

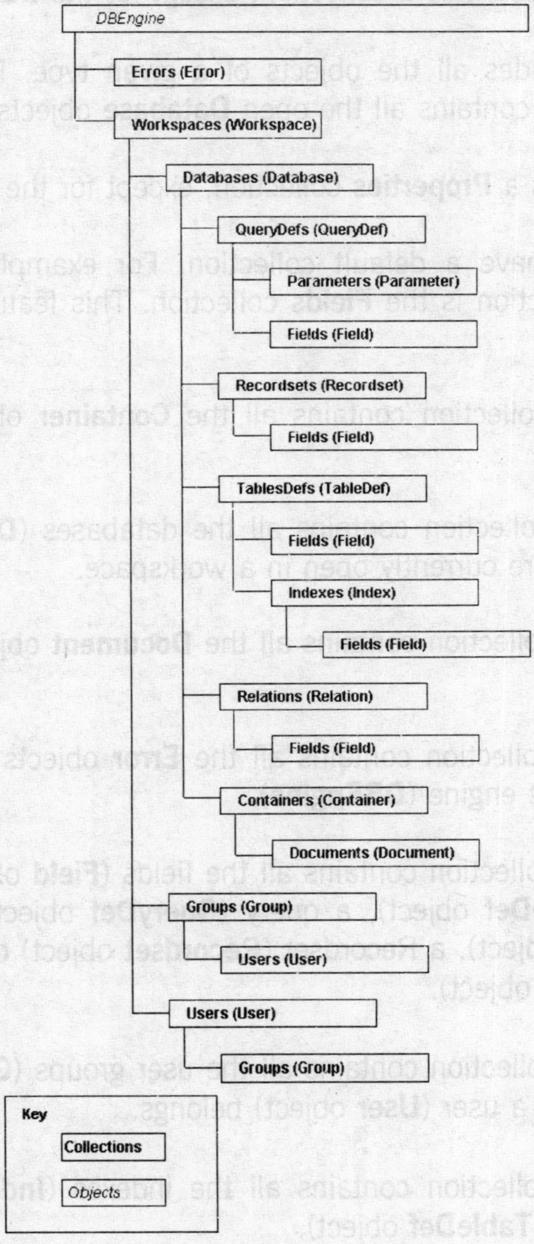

3. Collections

Each of the DAO objects has a collection, except for the **DBEngine** object.

Each collection includes all the objects of a given type. For example, the **Databases** collection contains all the open **Database** objects.

Each DAO object has a **Properties** collection, except for the **Error** object.

Most DAO objects have a default collection. For example the **Recordset** object's default collection is the **Fields** collection. This feature allows you to simplify your code.

Containers this collection contains all the **Container** objects in a database.

Databases this collection contains all the databases (**Database** objects) that are currently open in a workspace.

Documents this collection contains all the **Document** objects of a **Container**.

Errors this collection contains all the **Error** objects of the database access engine (**DBEngine**).

Fields this collection contains all the fields (**Field** objects) of a table (**TableDef** object), a query (**QueryDef** object), an index (**Index** object), a Recordset (**Recordset** object) or a relation (**Relation** object).

Groups this collection contains all the user groups (**Group** objects) to which a user (**User** object) belongs.

Indexes this collection contains all the indexes (**Index** objects) of a table (**TableDef** object).

Parameters this collection contains all the parameters (**Parameter** objects) of a query (**QueryDef** object).

Properties this collection contains all the properties (**Property** objects) of an object.

QueryDefs this collection contains all the query definitions (**QueryDef** objects) of a database (**Database** object).

Recordsets this collection contains all the recordsets (**Recordset** objects) that are currently open in a database (**Database** object).

Relations this collection contains all the relations (**Relation** objects) in a database (**Database** object).

TableDefs this collection contains all the table definitions (**TableDef** objects) in a database (**DataBase** object).

Users this collection contains all the users (**User** objects) in a workspace (**Workspace** object) or in a user group (**Group** object).

Workspaces this collection contains all the workspaces (**Workspace** objects) that are currently active.

Properties

Count returns the number of elements contained in the collection.

Item returns a specific collection member according to its position or its key.

All the collections can use these properties.

Example

This example lists the tables of the current database.

```
Dim intI As Integer
For intI = 0 To CurrentDb.TableDefs.Count - 1
   MsgBox CurrentDb.TableDefs.Item(intI).Name
Next intI
```

Methods

Append adds an object to a collection.

Delete removes an object from a collection.

Refresh refreshes the contents of a collection.

The **Errors**, **Databases**, **Containers**, **Documents**, **Parameters** and **Recordsets** collections cannot use the **Append** and **Delete** methods. The database engine manages the contents of these collections directly.

4. DBEngine object

This object represents the Microsoft Jet data access engine. It contains and controls all the other DAO objects.

Properties

DefaultType defines the type of workspace: Microsoft Jet or ODBCDirect.

DefaultUser and **DefaultPassword** — define the user name and password that the Microsoft Jet database engine uses when a Workspace object is created without a username or password.

InitPath — defines or returns information on the Windows registry key that contains values relative to the Microsoft Jet database engine.

SystemDB — defines or returns the access path to the current workgroup information file (this file has an .mdw name extension).

Version — returns the version number of the database or database engine that is associated with the object.

Methods

CompactDatabase — compresses a closed database.

CreateWorkspace — creates a new **Workspace** object.

Idle — interrupts processing to allow the Microsoft Jet database engine to finish any pending tasks.

SetOption — allows you to change the Microsoft Jet database engine options temporarily.

Collections

Workspaces, **Properties**, **Errors**

Examples

This example compresses the Employees database into the db1.mdb file.

```
DBEngine.CompactDatabase "c:\employees\employees.mdb", _
                    "c:\db1.mdb"
```

This example displays the version of the Microsoft Jet database engine.

```
MsgBox DBEngine.Version, vbExclamation, _
  "Microsoft Jet Engine Version number"
```

5. Workspace object

The **Workspace** object defines a work session for a user.

Properties

Name returns or defines the name of the Workspace object.

Type returns or defines the connection type of the Workspace object (dbUseJet constant, if the Workspace is connected to the Microsoft Jet database engine; dbUseODBC constant if the Workspace is connected to an ODBC data source).

UserName returns or defines the owner of the Workspace object.

Other properties

DefaultCursorDriver, IsolateODBCTrans, LoginTimeout.

Methods

BeginTrans starts a new transaction.

Close closes the **Workspace**.

CommitTrans closes the current transaction and saves the changes it has made.

CreateDatabase creates a new **Database** object.

CreateGroup creates a new user group.

CreateUser creates a new user.

OpenDatabase opens a database.

RollBack cancels the current transaction.

Collections

Databases, **Users**, **Groups**, **Properties**

Example

This example opens the Invoices database in the active workspace.

```
Dim wrk As Workspace
Dim dbs As Database
Set wrk = DBEngine.Workspaces(0)
Set dbs = wrk.OpenDatabase("C:\invoices\invoices.mdb")
```

6. Database object

The **Database** object represents an open database.

Properties

CollatingOrder	returns the method of comparing strings according to the language used.
Connect	returns or defines information needed to open an external database or to attach a table from an external database.
DesignMasterID	returns or defines the GUID of the Design master in a replica set.
Name	returns or defines the name of the database.
RecordsAffected	indicates the number of records affected the last time the **Execute** method ran.
Replicable	indicates whether or not the database can be replicated.
ReplicaID	returns the identifier of a replica.
Transactions	indicates whether or not a database supports transactions (ODBCDirect).
Updatable	indicates whether or not you can change a database object.
Version	returns the current DAO version.

V1xNullBehavior	indicates whether or not zero-length strings are converted to **Null** type values.

Methods

Close	closes the **Database** object.
CreateProperty	creates a new **Property** object.
CreateQueryDef	creates a new **QueryDef** object.
CreateRelation	creates a new **Relation** object.
CreateTableDef	creates a new **TableDef** object.
Execute	runs an action query or an SQL statement.
MakeReplica	creates a replica of the database.
NewPassword	defines a new password for a user account or a Microsoft Jet database.
OpenRecordset	creates a new **Recordset** object.
PopulatePartial	synchronizes any changes made in a partial replica with respect to the full replica.
Synchronize	synchronizes two replicas.

Collections

TableDefs, **QueryDefs**, **Relations**, **Containers**, **Recordsets**, **Properties**

Examples

This example sets up a reference to the current database.

```
Dim dbInvoices As DAO.Database
Set dbInvoices = CurrentDb()
```

This example opens an external database.

```
Dim dbsInvoices As DAO.Database
Set dbsInvoices = DBEngine.OpenDatabase _
("C:\Clients\Clients.mdb")
```

This example creates a RecordSet object in read-only mode from the Clients table in the current database.

```
Dim dbs As Database
Dim rstCli As DAO.Recordset
Set dbs = CurrentDb
Set rstCli = dbs.OpenRecordset("Clients", dbOpenTable, _
dbReadOnly)
```

7. Recordset object

The **Recordset** object contains records from a table or a query.

There are four main types of **Recordset** object:

Recordset	Description	Advantages	Declaration constant
Table	represents a table.	allows you to use indexes	dbOpenTable
Dynaset	represents the results of a query whose records can be updated.	allows you to work on data from several tables	dbOpenDynaset
ForwardOnly	similar to a Snapshot, except that you can only scroll forward through the records.	fast access	dbOpenForwardOnly
Snapshot	contains the results of a query in read-only mode.	provides faster access than the Dynaset type does.	dbOpenSnapshot

The Recordset object types concerned for each property or method are represented below by: **T** (Table), **D** (Dynaset), **S** (Snapshot) or **F** (ForwardOnly).

Properties

Recordset

Property	Description	Recordset
AbsolutePosition	returns or defines the position of a record in a recordset.	DS
BOF	indicates a position at the beginning of the **Recordset**.	DSTF
Bookmark	returns or defines a bookmark to identify a record uniquely.	DST
Bookmarkable	indicates whether or not the **Recordset** supports bookmarks.	DST
CacheStart	returns or defines the bookmark of the first record that must be locally cached.	D
DateCreated	returns the creation date and time of the underlying table.	T
EditMode	indicates the editing state of the current record.	DT
EOF	indicates a position at the end of the **Recordset**.	DSTF

Filter

defines the filter you want to apply. DSF

Index

defines the index you want to use. T

LockEdits

defines the type of edit locking you want to apply. DTS

LastModified

returns a bookmark indicating the last record that was changed. DT

LastUpdated

returns the date and time of the last change that was made to the underlying table. T

Name

returns the name of the **Recordset**. DSTF

NoMatch

indicates whether or not a specific record has been found. DST

PercentPosition

returns the current position of a record as a percentage of the total number of records. DST

RecordCount

returns the number of records assessed. DSTF

Restartable

indicates whether or not a **Recordset** supports the **Requery** method that reruns the underlying query. DSFT

Sort

defines the sort order. DS

Transactions

indicates whether or not a **Recordset** supports transactions. DTSF

Type

indicates the type of a **Recordset**. DSTF

Updatable

indicates whether or not you can change a DAO object. DTSF

ValidationText

specifies the error message that must appear if the validation condition is false. DSTF

ValidationRule

specifies the validation condition for the **Recordset**. DSTF

Methods

AddNew

creates a new record. DT

CancelUpdate

cancels any pending updates. DT

Clone

creates a copy of the **Recordset**. DST

Close

closes the **Recordset**. DSTF

CopyQueryDef

creates a copy of the **QueryDef** object associated with the **Recordset**. DSF

Delete

deletes the current record. DT

Edit

puts the current record in Edit mode. DT

FindFirst

finds the first record that meets a specific criterion and makes it the current record. DS

FindLast

finds the last record that meets a specific criterion and makes it the current record. DS

FindNext

finds the next record that meets a specific criterion and makes it the current record. DS

FindPrevious

finds the previous record that meets a specific criterion and makes it the current record. DS

GetRows

extracts rows from a Recordset and writes them into an array. DSTF

MoveFirst

moves to the first record in a Recordset and makes it the current record. DST

MoveLast

moves to the last record in a Recordset and makes it the current record. DST

MoveNext

moves to the next record in a Recordset and makes it the current record. DST

MovePrevious

moves to the previous record in a Recordset and makes it the current record. DST

Move

changes the position of the current record. DST

OpenRecordset

creates a new **Recordset**. DST

Requery

reruns the underlying query to update the records of a **Recordset**. DST

Seek

finds, with respect to a selected **Index**, the first record that meets a specific criterion and makes it the current record. T

Update

updates a record. DT

Examples

This example sets to uppercase the characters in the Cli_Company field of the Clients table.

```
Dim dbs As Database
Dim rstCli As DAO.Recordset

' Creating the Recordset
Set dbs = CurrentDb
Set rstCli = dbs.OpenRecordset("Clients", dbOpenTable)
rstCli.MoveFirst

' Scrolling through the records
With rstCli
  Do Until .EOF
      .Edit
      rstCli("Cli_Company") = UCase(rstCli("Cli_Company"))

      ' Updating
      .Update                                          .../...
```

```
.../...
      ' Next record
      .MoveNext
   Loop
End With
rstCli.Close
```

*This example uses the **Seek** method to find a client using a specific client code.*

```
Dim dbs As Database
Dim rstCli As DAO.Recordset
Dim strCliCode As String

' Creating the Recordset
Set dbs = CurrentDb
Set rstCli = dbs.OpenRecordset("Clients", dbOpenTable)
With rstCli
    ' Entering the client code
    strCliCode = InputBox("Enter the client code")
    ' Current Index: primary key
    .index = "PrimaryKey"
    ' Searching
    .Seek "=", strCliCode
    If .NoMatch Then
        ' Record not found
        MsgBox "Client not found"
    Else
        ' Record found
        MsgBox "Company: " & rstCli("Cli_Company")
    End If
End With
rstCli.Close
```

*This example uses the **Find** method to find a client whose Company name begins with a specific string.*

```
Dim dbs As DAO.Database
Dim rstCli As DAO.Recordset
Dim strCom As String
Dim strCrit As String

' Creating the Recordset
Set dbs = CurrentDb
Set rstCli = dbs.OpenRecordset("Clients", dbOpenSnapshot)
With rstCli
    ' Entering the beginning of the Company name
    strCom = InputBox _
    ("Enter the first letters of the Company name")
    .MoveLast
    ' Searching
    strCrit = "Cli_Company Like '" & strCom & "*'"
    .FindFirst strCrit
    If .NoMatch Then
        ' Record not found
        MsgBox "Client not found"
    Else
        ' If found: find any other clients
        Do While True
            MsgBox rstCli("Cli_Company")
            .FindNext strCrit
            If .NoMatch Then Exit Do
        Loop
    End If
End With
```

8. Tabledef object

The **Tabledef** object contains the stored definition of a base table or of a linked table in an external database.

Properties

Attributes	determines the characteristics of the table that the **TableDef** object describes (exclusivity, attachment, system, etc.).
ConflictTable	returns the name of the conflict table; this table contains any records that conflicted during the synchronization.
Connect	returns information on the source of the **TableDef** object.
DateCreated	indicates the date and time that the underlying table was created.
KeepLocal	determines whether or not a table must be replicated when the database is replicated.
LastUpdated	returns the date and time of the last change that was made to the underlying table.
Name	returns the name of the table.
RecordCount	returns the number of records in the table.
Replicable	indicates whether or not the table can be replicated.
ReplicaFilter	defines the records in a table that must be replicated.

SourceTableName specifies the name of the linked table.

Updatable indicates whether or not you can change a DAO object.

ValidationText specifies the error message that must appear if the validation condition is false.

ValidationRule specifies the validation condition for the object.

Methods

CreateField creates a new **Field**.

CreateIndex creates a new **Index**.

CreateProperty creates a new **Property** object.

OpenRecordset creates a new **Recordset** object.

RefreshLink refreshes information for a linked table.

Collections

Fields, **Indexes**, **Properties**.

Example

This example adds a Memo type field in the Clients table.

```
Dim dbs As DAO.Database
Dim tdf As DAO.TableDef
Dim fld As DAO.Field
Set dbs = CurrentDb
Set tdf = dbs.TableDefs("Clients")
Set fld = tdf.CreateField("Cli_Comment", dbMemo)
tdf.Fields.Append fld
```

9. Field and Index objects

➔ Field

A **Field** object represents a field in a table (**TableDef**), in a relation (**Relation**), in a query (**QueryDef**), in a recordset (**Recordset**) or in an index (**Index**).

Properties

AllowZeroLength specifies or returns whether or not the field supports a zero-length string.

Attributes defines or returns one or more characteristics of a field.

CollatingOrder returns characteristics for comparing strings and for the sort order.

DataUpdatable indicates whether or not a field can be updated.

DefaultValue	defines the default value of a field.
FieldSize	returns the size of a **Memo** field or a Long Binary field (**OLE Object**).
ForeignName	specifies, in a **Relation**, the name of the field in an external (foreign) table that corresponds to a field in the source (primary) table.
Name	returns or defines the name of a field.
OrdinalPosition	specifies the order in which the fields must be displayed.
Required	indicates whether or not a field must contain a value.
Size	returns or defines the size of a field.
SourceField	indicates the name of the data source field.
SourceTable	indicates the name of the data source table.
Type	indicates the data type of the field.
Value	defines or returns the value of a field.
ValidationText	specifies the error message that must appear if the validation condition is false.
ValidationOnSet	specifies whether or not a field value is validated immediately on modification.
ValidationRule	specifies the validation condition for the field.

Methods

AppendChunk adds data from a string expression to a **Memo** or Long Binary (**OLE object**) field.

CreateProperty creates a new **Property** object.

GetChunk reads all or part of a **Memo** or Long Binary (**OLE object**) field.

Collections

Properties

Example

This example lists the names and types of all the fields in the Clients table.

```
Dim dbs As DAO.Database
Dim tdf As DAO.TableDef
Dim fld As DAO.Field
Set dbs = CurrentDb
Set tdf = dbs.TableDefs("Clients")
For Each fld In tdf.Fields
    Debug.Print fld.Name & " " & fld.Type
Next
```

➔ Index

An **Index** object represents an index associated with a **TableDef** object or with a **Recordset** from a table.

Properties

Clustered	indicates whether or not the index represents a clustered index to a table.
DistinctCount	returns the number of unique values for an index in its associated table.
Foreign	indicates whether or not the index is a foreign key of the table.
IgnoreNulls	indicates whether or not index entries must be created for records whose index fields contain **Null** values.
Name	indicates the name of an index.
Primary	indicates if the index is the primary key.
Required	indicates whether or not all the fields in an index must contain a value.
Unique	indicates whether or not all the index values must be unique.

Methods

CreateField	creates a new field for an index.
CreateProperty	creates a new **Property** object.

Collections

Fields, Properties.

Example

This example creates the Company index to the Cli_Company field of the Clients table.

```
Dim dbs As DAO.Database
Dim tdf As DAO.TableDef
Dim fld As DAO.Field
Dim idx As DAO.Index

Set dbs = CurrentDb
Set tdf = dbs.TableDefs("Clients")
Set idx = tdf.CreateIndex("Company")
Set fld = idx.CreateField("Cli_Company")
idx.Unique = False
idx.Fields.Append fld
tdf.Indexes.Append idx
```

10.QueryDef and Parameter objects

→ QueryDef

A **QueryDef** object represents a stored definition of a query in a database.

Properties

Connect provides information on the database that the query uses.

DateCreated indicates the date and time the query was created.

KeepLocal indicates whether or not the query must be replicated.

LastUpdated indicates the date and time of the last change that was made to the query.

MaxRecords defines the maximum number of records that the query can return.

Name returns the name of the query.

RecordsAffected indicates the number of records affected the last time the **Execute** method ran.

Replicable indicates whether or not the query can be replicated.

ReturnsRecords indicates whether or not the query returns records.

SQL defines or returns the SQL statement associated with the query.

Type defines the type of the query (such as Select, Append or Delete, for example).

Updatable indicates whether or not you can change the query definition.

Methods

Close closes the query.

CreateProperty creates a new property.

Execute runs an action query or an SQL statement.

OpenRecordset creates a new **Recordset**.

Collections

Fields, Parameters, Properties

Examples

This example creates a new SQL-based query.

```
Dim dbs As Database
Dim qdf As QueryDef

Set dbs = CurrentDb
Set qdf = dbs.CreateQueryDef("List of employees sorted" _
& "by category")
qdf.SQL = "Select * from Employees Order by Categories;"
```

➔ Parameter

A **Parameter** object represents a parameter associated with a **QueryDef** object created from a parameter query.

Properties

Name	returns the name of the parameter.
Type	defines the data type of the parameter.
Value	defines or returns the value of the parameter.

Collections

Properties

Examples

This example creates a parameter query and displays how many parameters it uses.

```
Dim dbs As Database
Dim qdf As QueryDef
Dim par As Parameter
Set dbs = CurrentDb
Set qdf = dbs.CreateQueryDef("Employees " _
        & "in a category with " _
        & "category minimum salary")
qdf.SQL = "Select * from Employees Where (Category =" _
        & "[Enter the category] and Salary >=" _
        & "[Enter the minimum salary]);"
MsgBox qdf.Parameters.Count
```

11.Relation object

The **Relation** object represents a relationship between the fields of two **TableDef** or **QueryDef** objects.

Properties

Attributes determines the characteristics of the relation (one-to-one, referential integrity, etc.).

ForeignTable defines or returns the name of a foreign table.

Name defines or returns the name of the relation.

PartialReplica indicates whether or not the relation must be used to populate a partial replica from a full replica.

Table defines or returns the name of the **TableDef** or **QueryDef** source object.

Methods

CreateField creates a new **Field**.

Collections

Fields, Properties.

Example

This example stores different relations in a table, together with their properties. The Relations table contains three text fields (Rel_Source, Rel_Foreign and Rel_Type) and three Boolean fields (Rel_Integrity, Rel_Upd_Cascade and Rel_Del_Cascade).

```
Dim dbs As DAO.Database
Dim rst As DAO.Recordset
Dim rel As Relation
Dim intI As Integer

' Creating the Recordset
Set dbs = CurrentDb
Set rst = dbs.OpenRecordset("Relations", dbOpenTable)     .../...
```

```
.../...
' Storing the different relations of the relational model
' in the Relations table
For Each rel In dbs.Relations
    rst.AddNew
    rst("REL_Source") = rel.Table
    rst("Rel_Foreign") = rel.ForeignTable
    If rel.Attributes And dbRelationUnique Then
        rst("Rel_Type") = "1 to 1"
    Else
        rst("Rel_Type") = "1 to n"
    End If

    rst("Rel_Integrity") = IIf(rel.Attributes And _
        dbRelationDontEnforce, False, True)
    rst("Rel_Upd_Cascade") = IIf(rel.Attributes And _
        dbRelationUpdateCascade, True, False)
    rst("Rel_Del_Cascade") = IIf(rel.Attributes And _
        dbRelationDeleteCascade, True, False)
    rst.Update

Next
rst.Close
```

12.Container and Document objects

→ Container

A **Container** object groups together similar types of **Document** objects from a database.

Properties

AllPermissions returns all the permissions that apply to the **UserName** property of the current Container object.

Inherit indicates whether or not new **Document** objects inherit a default **Permissions** property value.

Name indicates the name of the container.

Owner indicates the owner of the container.

Permissions defines the permissions of a user or a group of users that the **UserName** property of the Container object identifies.

UserName defines the name of the user.

Example

This example lists the names of all the Container objects in a database.

```
Dim dbs As DAO.Database
Set dbs = CurrentDb
Dim ctn As Container

For Each ctn In dbs.Containers
    Debug.Print ctn.Name
Next
```

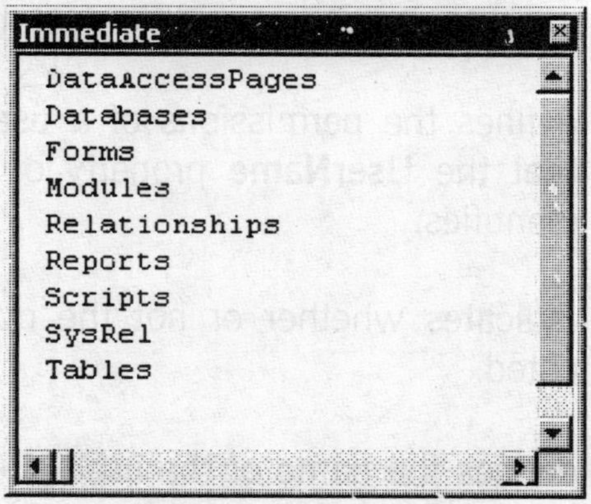

➔ Document

A **Document** object contains information on an instance of an object (database, saved table, query or relation).

Properties

AllPermissions returns all the permissions that apply to the **UserName** property of the current **Document** object.

Container returns the name of the **Container** object to which the **Document** object belongs.

DateCreated returns the date and time at which the underlying table was created.

KeepLocal determines whether or not a document must be replicated with the database.

LastUpdated returns the date and time of the last change made to the underlying table.

Name indicates the name of the document.

Owner indicates the owner of the document.

Permissions defines the permissions of a user or a group of users that the **UserName** property of the **Document** object identifies.

Replicable indicates whether or not the document can be replicated.

UserName defines the name of the user.

Collections

Properties

Example

This example lists all the data access pages.

```
Dim dbs As DAO.Database
Dim ctn As Container
Dim doc As Document

Set dbs = CurrentDb
For Each ctn In dbs.Containers
    If ctn.Name = "DataAccessPages" Then
        For Each doc In ctn.Documents
            Debug.Print doc.Name
        Next
    End If
Next
```

13.User and Group objects

→ User

A **User** object represents a user account with its permissions.

Properties

Name	indicates the name of the user account.
PID	indicates the personal identifier of the user account.
Password	defines the password of the user account.

Methods

CreateGroup	creates a new **Group** object.
NewPassword	defines a new password for the user.

Collections

Groups, **Properties**

→ Group

The **Group** object represents a group of users who have the same permissions.

Properties

Name indicates the name of the user group.

PID indicates the personal identifier of the user group.

Methods

CreateUser creates a new **User** object.

Collections

Users, **Properties**

Example

*This example displays, in the **Immediate** window, the users and groups that each group contains.*

```
Dim wrk As Workspace
Dim usr As User
Dim grp As Group

Set wrk = DBEngine.Workspaces(0)
For Each grp In wrk.Groups
    Debug.Print grp.Name
    With grp
        For Each usr In .Users
            Debug.Print usr.Name
        Next
    End With
Next
```

14.Error object

The **Error** object contains details on data access errors.

Properties

Description returns the error text.

HelpContext returns a contextual help identifier as a string variable: this ID corresponds to a topic in the Microsoft Windows Help file.

HelpFile indicates the fully qualified access path to the Help file.

Number returns the error number.

Source indicates the name of the object or application that generated the error.

Example

This example deliberately provokes an error and displays all the properties of the Error object.

```
On Error GoTo Error_handling

    ' Provoking an error
    ' The database NoDB.mdb does not exist
    DBEngine.Workspaces(0).OpenDatabase _
    ("C:\Invoices\NoDB.mdb")
    Exit Sub
                                              .../...
```

```
.../...
Error_handling:
    Dim strError As String
    Dim errLoop As Variant
' Scrolling through the elements of the Errors collection
' and displaying the properties of each Error object.
    For Each errLoop In Errors
        With errLoop
            strError = _
                "Error #" & .Number & vbCr
            strError = strError & _
                " " & .Description & vbCr
            strError = strError & _
                "(Source: " & .Source & ")" & vbCr
            strError = strError & _
                "Press F1 to display " & _
                "the Help topic" & .HelpContext & vbCr
            strError = strError & _
                " in the " & .HelpFile &" file."
        End With
        MsgBox strError
    Next
```

15.Property object

A **Property** object represents a property of an object.

Properties

Inherited indicates whether or not a property is inherited.

Name defines or returns the name of the property.

Type defines or returns the data type of the property.

Value defines or returns the value of the property.

Example

*This example displays, in the **Immediate** window, the name and value of each property in a Recordset object.*

```
Dim dbs As DAO.Database
Dim rst As DAO.Recordset
Dim prp As DAO.Property
Set dbs = CurrentDb
Set rst = dbs.OpenRecordset("Clients")
' scrolling through the properties
For Each prp In rst.Properties
   On Error Resume Next
   Debug.Print prp.Name & ": " & prp.Value
Next
```

C. ADO data access model

1. Introduction

The ADO (*ActiveX Data Objects*) object library allows you to write an application that accesses data on a database server and handle them via an OLE DB provider.

ADO is efficient, easy to use and does not require very much memory or disk space. ADO provides basic features for creating client/server and Web applications.

To use the ADO object library, you must tick the **Microsoft ActiveX Data Objects 2.x Library** reference in the object library reference list. If this reference is not available in this list, you must select the MSADO15.dll file, using the **Browse** button. This file generally resides in the folder C:\Program Files\Common Files\System\ADO.

You can also use the ADO extensions by activating the **Microsoft ADO Ext 2.x for DLL and Security** reference (from the MSADOX.dll file). These extensions provide access to complementary ADO objects (such as catalog, users and views, for example).

The ADO210.chm help file provides detailed explanations on using the ADO model.

2. ADO and OLE DB

OLE DB technology allows you to access data stored in different information sources: relational and non-relational databases, messaging systems, file systems and so on. You can access practically all company data using OLE DB.

ADO (ActiveX Data Objects) is the programming interface that allows you to access the information from all OLE DB data providers.

Technological architecture

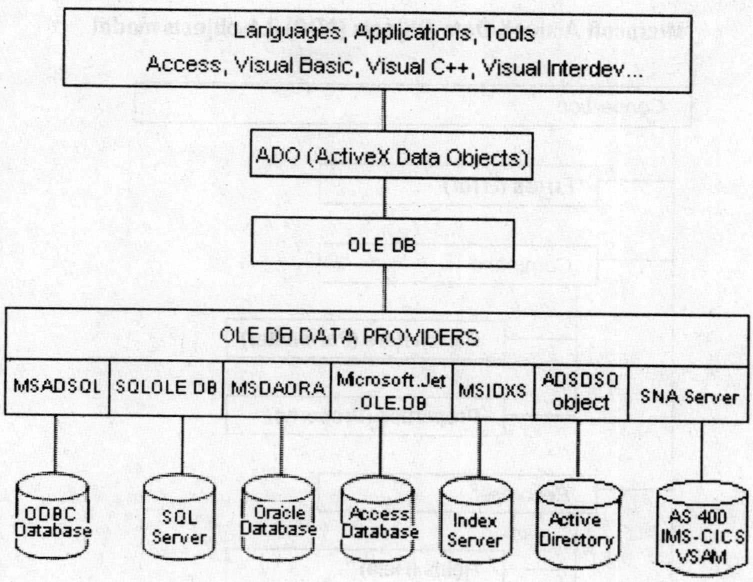

The data Providers are drivers that allow you to communicate with the data sources.

3. ADO objects hierarchy

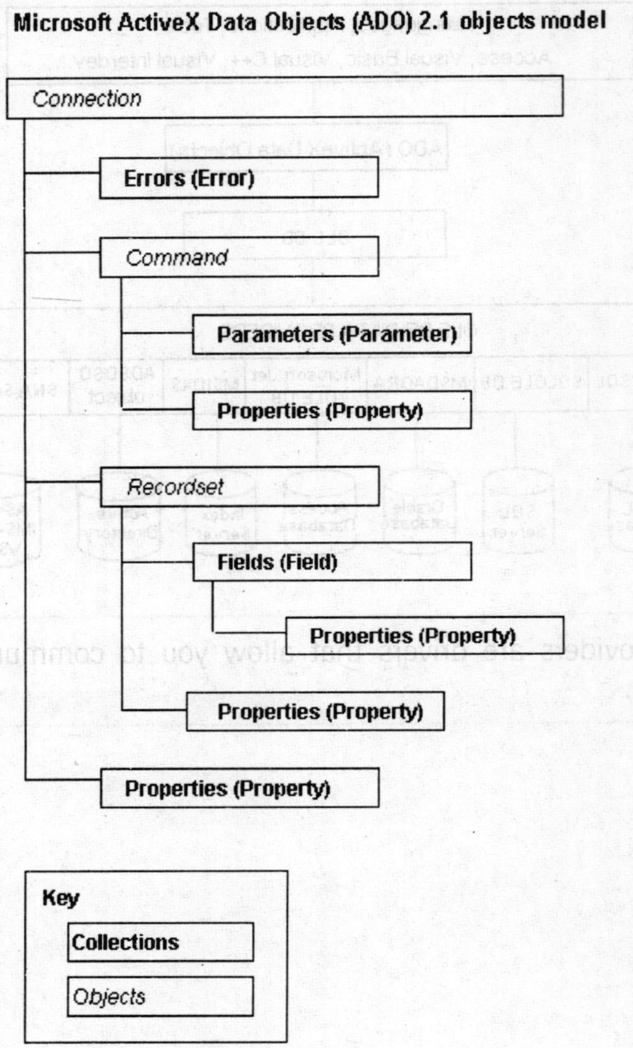

4. ADO programming model

ADO allows you to run the following actions:

- connect to an OLE BD or ODBC database, using the Connection object.
- create a command to send an SQL statement to the server, using the Command object.
- run the command and store any data returned by the command in the Recordset object.
- process the data in the Recordset object: to sort, filter, modify or delete the records, for example.
- update the data: to validate any changes made to the Recordset object and incorporate the changes in a transaction.
- accept or refuse any updates specified during a transaction.

Example

```
Dim cnn As New ADODB.Connection
Dim cmd As New ADODB.Command
Dim rs  As New ADODB.Recordset

' Step 1: connecting to an SQL Server data source
' using OLE DB technology
cnn.Open "Provider=SQLOLDB.1;Data Source=SRV;" _
        & "Initial Catalog=Invoices;" _
        & "Integrated Security=SSPI;" _
        & "Persist Security Info=False;"

' Step 2: creating a command
Set cmd.ActiveConnection = cnn
cmd.CommandText = "SELECT * FROM Clients"
                                                  .../...
```

```
.../...
' Step 3: running the command
rs.CursorLocation = adUseClient
rs.Open cmd, , adOpenStatic, adLockBatchOptimistic

' Step 4: handling the data
rs.Filter = "City LIKE 'Portsmouth'"
Do While Not rs.EOF
    rs("Country") = "UK"
    rs.MoveNext
Loop

' Step 5: updating modified data
cnn.BeginTrans
rs.UpdateBatch

' Step 6: closing the update of the SQL database
If MsgBox("Confirm the changes?", vbYesNo) = vbYes
Then
    cnn.CommitTrans
Else
    cnn.RollbackTrans
End If
```

5. ADO objects

Connection represents a connection with a data source.

Command defines a specific command that will run on a data source.

Recordset represents the complete recordset of a database table or the results of a command (for example, the results of an SQL query).

6. ADO collections

Parameters this collection contains all the **Parameter** objects of a **Command** object. The **Parameter** object represents a parameter or argument associated with a **Command** object that is based on a parameterized query or a parameterized stored procedure.

Properties this collection contains all the **Property** objects of a given object (**Connection**, **Command** or **Recordset**). The **Property** object represents a dynamic characteristic of an ADO object defined by the user.

Errors this collection contains all the **Error** objects created upon a single failure concerning the OLE DB provider. Each **Error** object contains information on a specific data access error.

7. Connection objects

Methods

BeginTrans starts a new transaction.

Cancel cancels a current asynchronous **Execute** or **Open** method call.

Close closes an open object along with any objects that depend on it.

CommitTrans saves any modifications and closes the current transaction.

Execute runs the query, SQL statement, stored procedure or text specific to the OLE DB provider.

Open opens a connection to a data source to run commands on it.

OpenSchema gets database information from the OLE DB provider.

RollbackTrans cancels any data modifications made by the current transaction and closes the current transaction.

Properties

Attributes defines or returns one or more characteristics of a **Connection** object; the default value is zero.

CommandTimeout indicates the length of time a command can run before the system interrupts the attempt and generates an error message; the default value is 30 seconds.

ConnectionString defines or returns the information used to set up a connection with a data source.

ConnectionTimeout indicates the length of time the system will wait for a connection to set up before it interrupts the attempt and generates an error message; the default value is 15 seconds.

CursorLocation defines or returns the location of the cursor service for a connection (a client-side cursor or a server-side cursor).

DefaultDatabase indicates the default database for a **Connection** object.

IsolationLevel indicates the isolation level of a **Connection** object.

Mode indicates the permissions of a **Connection** object to modify data.

Provider indicates the name of an OLE DB provider for a **Connection** object.

State indicates whether a **Connection** object is open or closed (this property is read-only).

Version indicates the ADO version number (this property is read-only).

Examples

This example sets up a reference to the current database:

```
Dim cncInvoices As ADODB.Connection
Set cncInvoices = CurrentProject.Connection
```

This example opens an external database:

```
Dim cncInvoices As ADODB.Connection
Set cncInvoices = New ADODB.Connection
cncInvoices.Open "Provider=Microsoft.Jet.OLEDB.4.0.;" _
        & "Data Source = C:\Invoices\Invoices.mdb"
```

This example uses the CommitTrans and RollbackTrans methods to confirm and to cancel record updates, respectively:

```
Dim cnc As ADODB.Connection
Dim strSQL As String
Dim strMessage As String

' Opening the connection
Set cnc = CurrentProject.Connection

' Starting the transaction
cnc.BeginTrans

' SQL update queries
strSQL = "UPDATE CLIENTS SET CLI_COUNTRY = 'England'" _
      & "WHERE CLI_CITY = 'Bristol'"
cnc.Execute strSQL
strSQL = "UPDATE CLIENTS SET CLI_COUNTRY = 'Canada'" _
      & "WHERE CLI_CITY = 'Vancouver'"
cnc.Execute strSQL

' Asking the user to validate his/her changes
If MsgBox("Confirm your changes?", vbYesNo) _
    = vbYes Then
    ' Saving the changes
    cnc.CommitTrans
Else
    ' Cancelling the changes
    cnc.RollbackTrans
End If
cnc.Close
```

8. Command object

Methods

Cancel	cancels a pending asynchronous **Execute** or **Open** method call.
CreateParameter	creates a new **Parameter** object and specifies its properties.
Execute	runs the query, SQL statement or stored procedure that the **CommandText** property specifies.

Properties

ActiveConnection	indicates the **Connection** object associated with the command.
CommandText	contains the text of the command to be issued to an OLE DB provider.
CommandTimeout	indicates the length of time a command can run before the system interrupts the attempt and generates an error message; the default value is 30 seconds.
CommandType	indicates the type of the **Command** object.
Name	indicates the name of the **Command** object.
Prepared	indicates whether or not a compiled version of a command must be saved before it runs.

State indicates whether a **Connection** object is open or closed (this property is read-only).

Examples

This example uses the Command object to create a recordset.

```
Dim cnc As New ADODB.Connection
Dim cmd As New ADODB.Command
Dim rst As New ADODB.Recordset

' Opening the connection
cnc.Open "Provider=Microsoft.Jet.OLEDB.4.0.;" _
        & "Data Source = C:\Invoices\Invoices2.mdb"

' Running the command
Set cmd.ActiveConnection = cnc
cmd.CommandType = adCmdText
cmd.CommandText _
    = "SELECT * FROM CLIENTS WHERE CLI_City = 'Bristol'"
Set rst = cmd.Execute

' Listing the records
Do While Not rst.EOF
    Debug.Print rst("CLI_Company")
    rst.MoveNext
Loop
rst.Close
cnc.Close
```

9. Recordset object

Methods

AddNew creates a new record for an updatable **Recordset** object.

Cancel cancels a current asynchronous **Open** method call.

CancelBatch cancels a pending batch update.

CancelUpdate cancels any modifications being made to a current or new row of a recordset before the **Update** method has been called.

Clone duplicates an existing **Recordset** object.

Close closes the **Recordset** object along with all the objects that depend on it.

CompareBookmarks compares two bookmarks and indicates their relative positions.

Delete deletes the current record(s).

Find searches a **Recordset** object that corresponds to specific criteria.

GetRows extracts several rows of a **Recordset** object and puts them in an array.

GetString returns a **Recordset** object in the form of a string.

Move moves the current record to a new position in the **Recordset** object.

MoveFirst moves the current record to the first position in the **Recordset** object.

MoveLast moves the current record to the last position in the **Recordset** object.

MoveNext moves the current record to the next position in the **Recordset** object.

MovePrevious moves the current record to its previous position in the **Recordset** object.

NextRecordset returns the next recordset (for a command that contains several extraction queries).

Open opens a cursor to the records in an array or to the results of a query.

Requery updates the **Recordset** object by rerunning the query on which the object is based.

Resync refreshes the data in the current **Recordset** object from the information in the underlying database.

Save saves the **Recordset** object in a file.

Seek searches the index of a **Recordset** object for a row that corresponds to a value and uses it to replace the current row (this is a new feature of ADO 2.1).

Supports determines whether or not a **Recordset** object supports a particular feature.

Update saves the changes made to the current row of a **Recordset** object.

UpdateBatch saves current batch updates to disk.

Properties

AbsolutePage indicates the page that contains the current record.

AbsolutePosition indicates the ordinal position of the current row of a **Recordset** object.

ActiveCommand indicates the **Command** object that created the associated **Recordset** object (this property is read-only).

ActiveConnection indicates the **Connection** object to which a **Recordset** belongs.

BOF indicates that the current record is positioned before the first record of the **Recordset** object (this property is read-only).

Bookmark returns a bookmark that uniquely identifies the current row in a **Recordset** object or associates the current row with a record that a valid bookmark identifies.

CacheSize indicates the number of records from a **Recordset** object that the cache memory stores.

CursorLocation defines or returns the location of the cursor service (client side or server side).

CursorType indicates the type of cursor used with a **Recordset** object.

DataMember indicates the name of the data member to be extracted from the object that the **DataSource** property defines (this property is read-only).

DataSource indicates that an object contains data that must be represented as a **Recordset** object (this property is read-only).

EditMode indicates the editing status of the current record (this property is read-only).

EOF indicates that the current record is positioned after the last record of the **Recordset** object (this property is read-only).

Filter defines a data filter in the **Recordset**.

Index indicates the name of the current index for the **Recordset**.

LockType indicates the type of locks that are applied to records when they are being modified.

MarshalOptions indicates the records that must be marshaled back to the server.

MaxRecords indicates the maximum number of records that can be returned to a **Recordset** object from the same query; there is no upper limit to this value, which defaults to zero.

PageCount indicates the number of data pages that the **Recordset** object contains (this property is read-only).

PageSize indicates the number of records that a **Recordset** page contains.

Properties references the **Collection** of **Property** objects of the current **Recordset** object.

RecordCount indicates the number of records that the **Recordset** object currently contains (this property is read-only).

Sort specifies one or more field names used to sort the **Recordset** object along with the sort order for each field.

Source indicates the source of the **Recordset** object.

State indicates the state of the **Recordset** object (open or closed) along with any current asynchronous operation (this property is read-only).

Status indicates the status of the current record with respect to batch updating or other global operations (this property is read-only).

StayInSync indicates, in the case of a hierarchical **Recordset** object, whether or not all the underlying child rows must change when the parent row changes (this property is read-only).

Examples

This example changes all the characters to uppercase in the Cli_Company field of the Clients table:

```
Dim cnc As New ADODB.Connection
Dim rstCli As New ADODB.Recordset

' Creating the Recordset
Set cnc = CurrentProject.Connection
rstCli.Open "Select * From Clients", cnc, adOpenKeyset, _
adLockOptimistic

' Scrolling through the records
With rstCli
    Do Until .EOF
        rstCli("Cli_Company") = UCase(rstCli("Cli_Company"))
        ' Updating
        .Update
        ' Next record
        .MoveNext
    Loop
End With
rstCli.Close
cnc.Close
```

*This example uses the **Seek** method to find a client by its code:*

```
Dim cnc As New ADODB.Connection
Dim rstCli As New ADODB.Recordset
Dim strCodeCli As String

' Creating the Recordset
Set cnc = CurrentProject.Connection
rstCli.Open "Clients", cnc, adOpenKeyset, adLockReadOnly, _
adCmdTableDirect

With rstCli
    ' Entering the client code
    strCodeCli = InputBox("Enter the client code")
    ' Current index: primary key
    .index = "PrimaryKey"
    ' Searching
    .Seek strCodeCli, adSeekFirstEQ
    If .EOF Then
        ' Record not found
        MsgBox "Client not found"
    Else
        ' Record found
        MsgBox "Company: " & rstCli("Cli_Company")
    End If
End With

rstCli.Close
cnc.Close
```

*This example uses the **Find** method to find the clients, the names of whose companies begin with a specific string:*

```
Dim cnc As New ADODB.Connection
Dim rstCli As New ADODB.Recordset
Dim strCie As String
Dim strCrit As String
Dim bkm As Variant

' Creating the Recordset
Set cnc = CurrentProject.Connection
rstCli.Open "Clients", cnc, adOpenKeyset, adLockReadOnly, _
            adCmdTableDirect
With rstCli
    ' Entering the client code
    strCie = _
    InputBox("Enter the first letters of the company name")
    ' Searching
    strCrit = "Cli_Company Like '" & strCie & "%'"
    .Find strCrit, , adSearchForward
    If .EOF Then
        ' Record not found
        MsgBox "Client not found"
    Else
        ' Record found: look for any others
        Do While Not .EOF
            MsgBox rstCli("Cli_Company")
            ' Current position
            bkm = .Bookmark
            .Find strCrit, 1, adSearchForward, bkm
        Loop
    End If
End With
rstCli.Close
cnc.Close
```

10.Fields collection

Methods

Append adds a **Field** object to a **Fields** collection.

Delete deletes a **Field** object from the **Fields** collection.

Refresh refreshes **Field** objects from the **Fields** collection.

11.Field object

Methods

AppendChunk adds data to a large text or binary **Field** object.

GetChunk returns part or all the contents of a large text or binary **Field** object.

Properties

ActualSize indicates the length of a **Field** (this property is read-only).

Attributes indicates one or more characteristics of a **Field** object.

DefinedSize indicates the size of a **Field** object (this property is read-only).

Name indicates the name of a **Field** object.

NumericScale indicates the scale of a **Field** object's numeric values (this property is read-only).

OriginalValue indicates the value of a **Field** object before modification (this property is read-only).

Precision indicates the level of precision for numeric values in the **Field** object (this property is read-only).

Properties contains all the **Property** objects of a **Field** object.

Type indicates the type of data in the **Field** object.

Underlying Value indicates the current value of a **Field** object in the database (this property is read-only).

Value indicates the value of a **Field** object.

12.Parameters collection

Methods

Append adds a **Parameter** object to a **Parameters** collection.

Delete deletes a **Parameter** object from the **Parameters** collection.

Refresh refreshes **Parameter** objects from the **Parameters** collection.

Example

This example lists all the fields of the Clients table.

```
Dim cnc As New ADODB.Connection
Dim rstCli As New ADODB.Recordset
Dim fld As ADODB.Field

' Creating the Recordset
Set cnc = CurrentProject.Connection
rstCli.Open "Clients", cnc, adOpenKeyset, adLockReadOnly, _
adCmdTableDirect
For Each fld In rstCli.Fields
    Debug.Print fld.Name & " " & fld.Type
Next
rstCli.Close
```

13.Parameter object

Methods

AppendChunk adds data to a large text or binary **Parameter** object.

Properties

Attributes indicates one or more characteristics of a **Parameter** object.

Direction indicates whether the **Parameter** object corresponds to an input parameter, to an output parameter, to both or to the return parameter of a stored procedure.

Name indicates the name of the **Parameter** object (this property is read-only).

NumericScale indicates the scale of a **Parameter** object's numeric values (this property is read-only).

Precision indicates the level of precision for numeric values in the **Parameter** object (this property is read-only).

Properties contains all the **Property** objects of a **Parameter** object.

Size indicates the maximum size in bytes or characters of a **Parameter** object.

Type indicates the type of data in the **Parameter** object.

Value indicates the value of a **Parameter** object.

14.Properties collection

Methods

Refresh refreshes **Property** objects from the **Properties** collection.

15. Property object

Properties

Attributes indicates one or more characteristics of a **Property** object.

Name indicates the name of the **Property** object (this property is read-only).

Type indicates the data type of the **Property** object (this property is read-only).

Value indicates the value of the **Property** object (this property is read-only).

16. Errors collection

Methods

Clear deletes all the **Error** objects from the **Errors** collection.

Refresh refreshes the **Error** objects from OLE DB provider information.

Properties

Count indicates the number of **Error** objects in the **Errors** collection (this property is read-only).

Item indicates a specific member of the **Errors** collection (this property is read-only).

17. Error object

Properties

Description returns the descriptive string associated with the **Error** object (this property is read-only).

HelpContext indicates the Help file **ContextID** for the associated **Error** object (this property is read-only).

HelpFile indicates the name of the Help file associated with the **Error** object (this property is read-only).

NativeError indicates the error code specific to the OLE DB provider for the **Error** object (this property is read-only).

Number indicates a unique identifier of the Error object (this property is read-only).

Source indicates the name of the object or application that provoked the error (this property is read-only).

SQLState indicates the SQL state of a given **Error** object, as a 5-character string in compliance to the ANSISQL standard (this property is read-only).

Chapter 5: SQL language

A. Introduction

You can use SQL (Structured Query Language) to query relational database management systems.

Access 2002 uses SQL as its query language. When you create a query in **Query Design View**, Access builds the equivalent set of SQL statements as a background task. In fact, most query properties in design view have equivalent clauses and options that you can access using the SQL language.

You can display and modify the SQL statement corresponding to a query by going into SQL view.

Example

Open an existing query in **Design** view.

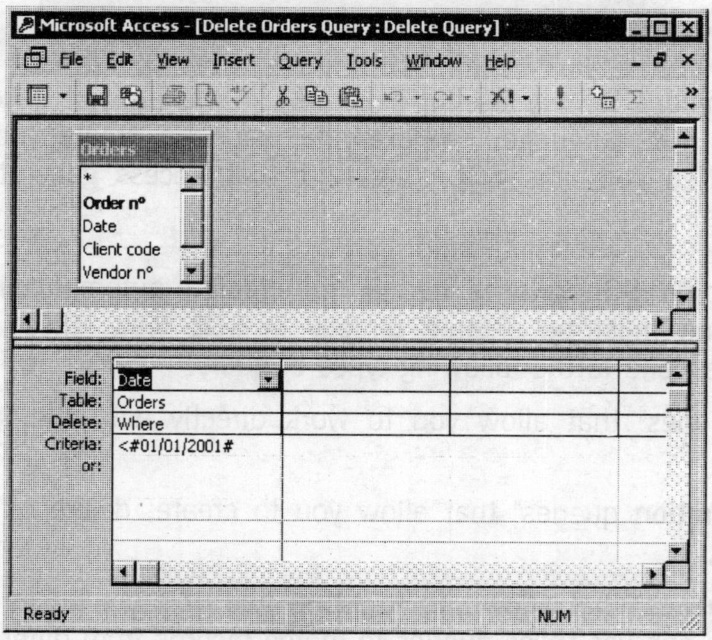

· Next, open the list on the **View** tool button and choose **SQL View**.

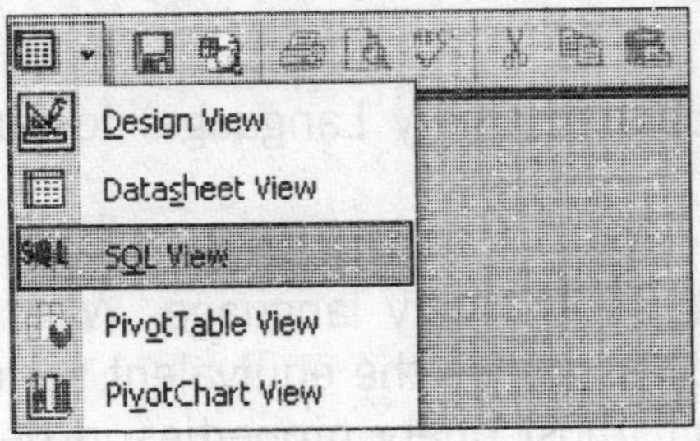

Access displays the SQL statement corresponding to your query.

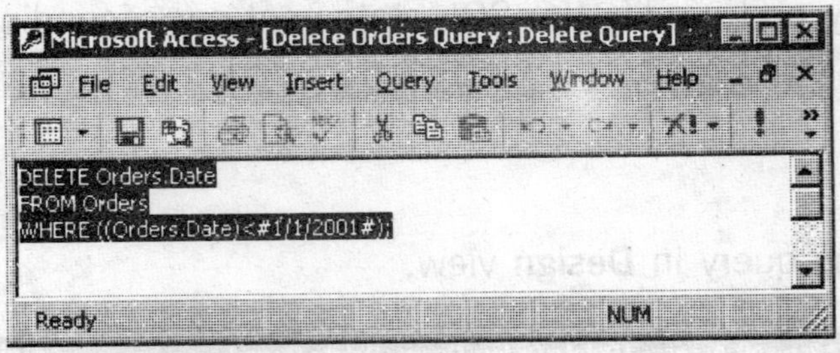

This technique is very useful, especially if you are not used to working with the SQL language. For example, you can create your queries in Access then copy the SQL statement that Access generates into your VBA code.

However, some SQL queries cannot be created automatically using this technique and must be entered directly in SQL view: these SQL-specific queries correspond to the following types of query:

- "**direct** queries" that allow you to work directly with the tables on the server,
- "**data definition** queries" that allow you to create, delete or modify table structures,
- "**Union** queries" that allow you to group two or more tables in the query result: you can use these queries to merge records from different tables.

B. SQL and VBA

SQL queries are totally compatible with VBA. You can use them via the methods of various objects, for example:

- the **OpenRecordset** method of the **DataBase** and **Connection** objects,
- the **CreateQueryDef** method of the **DataBase** and **Connection** objects,
- the **Execute** method of the **Command** and **Connection** objects...

You can also use SQL queries in forms and reports. For example:

- in the **RecordSource** property of a form or a report,
- in the **RowSource** property of a drop-down list.

You can modify most of these properties in your VBA code.

Using SQL statements in your VBA code, offers the following benefits:

Execution speed	for example, the **Select** statement runs quicker than the equivalent VBA statements for scrolling through a table,
Enhanced performance	in client/server mode, the DBMS pre-compiles the queries, which optimizes their performance,
Easy maintenance	SQL statements are shorter and more readable than their VBA equivalents,
Standardization	SQL is the standard query language for relational databases.

C. SQL statements

1. SELECT statement

SELECT is the most commonly used SQL statement: it corresponds to the Select query in Access. This statement extracts fields from a set of records that meet certain criteria.

Syntax

```
SELECT [ALL | DISTINCT] <Fieldlist>
FROM <Tablelist>
[WHERE... ]
[GROUP BY... ]
[HAVING.. ]
[ORDER BY... ]
```

`ALL` (default option) — includes all the records that meet the statement's criteria.

`DISTINCT` — omits records whose values are duplicated by other records.

<field list> specifies the different fields concerned: you must separate the fields by commas, using the following syntax:
* | table.* | [table.]field1 [AS alias1] [, [table.]field2 [AS alias2] [, ...]]

selects all fields from the specified tables.

`alias1, alias2`	specify column headers that must be used instead of the tables' original column headers.
`<table list>`	indicates the tables that contain the data you want to extract. If your query uses several tables, the FROM clause must specify the join mode.

Examples

- SELECT * FROM Products
- SELECT Products.* FROM Products
- SELECT Prod_code, Prod_desc, Prod_price, Prod_tax FROM Products

2. FROM clause

The FROM clause specifies the tables or the queries that contain the required data.

Syntax

```
FROM table1 [ LEFT | RIGHT | INNER ] JOIN table2 ON
table1.field1 <comparison operator> table2.field2
```

`[ LEFT | RIGHT | INNER ]`	define the type of join between the tables.
`LEFT JOIN`	creates a left outer join; when applied to two tables, a left outer join includes all the records in the first table (the left table: <table 1>), even those that have no corresponding values in the second table (the right table: <table 2>).

`RIGHT JOIN`	creates a right outer join; when applied to two tables, a right outer join includes all the records in the second table (the right table: <table 2>) even those that have no corresponding values in the first table (the left table: <table 1>).
`INNER JOIN`	includes only those records that contain identical data in link fields in both (or all) the tables.
`<comparison operator>`	can be any of the relational comparison operators such as =, <, >, <= or >= (the = operator is the most commonly used).

Examples

These examples list orders by company. The first example selects only those clients who have placed orders. The second example selects all the clients.

```
SELECT Clients.Cli_Company, Orders.Ord_DateOrd
FROM Clients INNER JOIN Orders ON
Clients.Cli_CodeCLi = Orders.Ord_CodeCli
```

```
SELECT Clients.Cli_Company, Orders.Ord_DateOrd
FROM Clients LEFT JOIN Orders ON
Clients.Cli_CodeCLi = Orders.Ord_CodeCli
```

3. WHERE clause

The WHERE clause filters the records according to specific criteria.

The WHERE clause conditions use the following operators:

- comparison operators: =, <, >, <=, >=, Is [Not] Null, [Not] In, Between.
- logical operators: And, Or, Not.

Examples

```
SELECT * FROM Products WHERE [Prod_Price ] >= 500
SELECT * FROM Products WHERE [Prod_Price]
        BETWEEN 100 AND 200
SELECT * FROM Clients WHERE [Cli_Country] IN
        ('England','Ireland','Canada')
```

4. GROUP BY clause

The GROUP BY clause calculates the "**totals**" in an Access query. It groups together one or more fields. It is used mainly to apply aggregate functions such as Sum, Count and Avg.

Examples

This query returns the number of orders that clients have placed:

```
SELECT Clients.Cli_Company, Count(Orders.Ord_OrdDate)
    AS NbOrders
FROM Clients
    LEFT JOIN Orders
    ON Clients.Cli_CliCode=Orders.Ord_CliCode
GROUP BY Clients.Cli_Company
```

This query returns the total amount for each of the orders:

```
SELECT Orders.Ord_OrdNum, Sum([Ord_Price]*[Ord_Qte])
    AS TotalOrd
FROM Orders
    INNER JOIN [Order details]
    ON Orders.Ord_OrdNum = [Order details].Ord_OrdNum
GROUP BY Orders.Ord_OrdNum
```

5. HAVING clause

The HAVING clause specifies the records that must be chosen by a SELECT statement that has a GROUP BY clause. The statement will select all the records specified by the GROUP BY clause that meet the criteria specified by the HAVING clause.

Example

This query extracts the orders whose total amounts exceed 20 000:

```
SELECT Orders.Ord_OrdNum, Sum(Ord_Price * Ord_Qte)
   AS TotalOrd, Orders.Ord_OrdDate
FROM Orders
   INNER JOIN [Order details]
   ON Orders.Ord_OrdNum = [Order details].Ord_OrdNum
GROUP BY Orders.Ord_OrdNum, Orders.Ord_OrdDate
HAVING (Sum(Ord_Price * Ord_Qte) > 20000)
```

6. ORDER BY clause

The ORDER BY clause sorts the query's result records in ascending or descending order according to the specified fields.

Syntax

```
[ORDER BY field1 [ASC|DESC][, field2 [ASC|DESC]][, ...]]]
```

`ASC` sorts in ascending order.

`DESC` sorts in descending order.

Example

This query returns the number of orders placed by clients, sorted on the number of orders in descending order.

```
SELECT Clients.Cli_Company, Count(Orders.Ord_OrdDate)
   AS NbOrders
FROM Clients
   LEFT JOIN Orders
   ON Clients.Cli_CliCode=Orders.Ord_CliCode
GROUP BY Clients.Cli_Company
ORDER BY Count(Orders.Ord_OrdDate) DESC
```

7. UPDATE statement

The UPDATE statement modifies a table's field values for records that meet any specified criteria.

Syntax

```
UPDATE table
SET field1 = new_value1, field2 = new_value2 ...
[WHERE criteria]
```

If you do not specify a Where clause, your UPDATE query will modify all the records in the table.

Example

This query changes the country code of all the records in the Clients table.

```
UPDATE Clients SET Clients.Cli_Country = 'UK'
```

This query changes the country code of all the records in the Clients table that correspond to the UK city of 'Portsmouth'.

```
UPDATE Clients SET Clients.Cli_Country = 'UK'
  WHERE Clients.Cli_City='Portsmouth'
```

8. DELETE statement

The DELETE statement deletes records from the table(s) indicated by the FROM clause, according to any specified criteria.

Syntax

```
DELETE FROM table
[WHERE criteria]
```

If you do not specify a Where clause, your DELETE query will delete all the records in the table.

Example

This query deletes all the orders that were placed before 2001:

```
DELETE Orders.Ord_OrdDate
FROM Orders
WHERE ((Orders.Ord_OrdDate)< #1/1/2001#)
```

9. INSERT INTO statement

The INSERT INTO statement adds records into a table (this corresponds to an Append query).

Syntax

This syntax adds a single record to a table:

```
INSERT INTO <DestinationTable> [(field1[, field2[, ...]])]
VALUES (value1[, value2[, ...]])
```

You must specify, in the same order and of the same type, as many values as there are fields to be filled.

This syntax adds several records to a table:

```
INSERT INTO <DestinationTable> [(field1[, field2[, ...]])]
SELECT [<SourceTable>.]field1[, field2[, ...]]
FROM <TableList>
```

The SELECT statement must return, in the same order and of the same type, as many values as there are fields to be filled (as specified by the first part of the statement).

Examples

This query adds a record into the Clients table:

```
INSERT INTO Clients (Cli_CodeCLi, Cli_Company, Cli_City, Cli_Country)
VALUES ('ENI', 'ENI Publishing', 'London', 'UK')
```

This query adds the records from the Prospects table into the Clients table:

```
INSERT INTO Clients
SELECT Prospects.*
FROM Prospects
```

10.Other statements

Extracting data

TRANSFORM creates a crosstab query.

UNION creates a query that merges the result of two or more independent queries or tables; the tables and/or queries you want to merge must have identical structures.

Creating and managing tables

CREATE TABLE creates a new table.

CREATE INDEX creates a new index for an existing table.

ALTER TABLE modifies the structure of a table.

DROP TABLE deletes a table from the database.

DROP INDEX deletes an index for a table.

Creating and managing users and user groups

CREATE USER	creates one or more users.
ADD USER	adds one or more users to an existing user group.
DROP USER	deletes one or more users.
CREATE GROUP	creates one or more user groups.
DROP GROUP	deletes one or more user groups.
GRANT	attributes specific permissions to an existing user or group.
REVOKE	withdraws specific permissions from an existing user or group.

For more information on the SQL language, consult the Microsoft Jet SQL Reference under the **Contents** tab of the Microsoft Access Help application.

D.SQL examples

To illustrate the usefulness of the SQL language, here are two equivalent procedures: one uses SQL and the other does not.
To run these examples, you must create a **Clients** table with a field called **Cli_Company** and create a few records in this table. Alternatively, you could import the **Customers** table from the **Northwind.mdb** sample database that Access 2002 provides and rename the fields, **CompanyName** as **Cli_Company**, **Country** as **Cli_Country** and **City** as **Cli_City**.

1. Updating records

This example changes the contents of a field in a table for the records that meet certain criteria.

Here is the example of VBA code with an SQL UPDATE query:

```
Private Sub Update_Country1()
Dim cncInvoices As ADODB.Connection
Dim strSQL As String

'   Updating the country code in the clients table
Set cncInvoices = CurrentProject.Connection
strSQL = "UPDATE Clients SET Clients.CLI_COUNTRY = 'UK' " _
   & "WHERE Clients.CLI_CITY='Westport'"
cncInvoices.Execute strSQL

End Sub
```

Here is the equivalent VBA code without an SQL query:

```
Private Sub Update_Country2()
Dim cncInvoices As ADODB.Connection
Dim rstClient As ADODB.Recordset

'   Opening a recordset
Set cncInvoices = CurrentProject.Connection
Set rstClient = New ADODB.Recordset
rstClient.Open "CLIENTS", cncInvoices, adOpenForwardOnly, _
adLockOptimistic

                                                   .../...
```

```
.../...
'   Scrolling through the Clients table
Do While Not rstClient.EOF
    If rstClient("CLI_CITY") = "Westport" Then
        rstClient("CLI_COUNTRY") = "UK"
        rstClient.Update
    End If
    rstClient.MoveNext
Loop

End Sub
```

2. Loading a drop-down list

This example displays, in a drop-down list box control, the name of the clients whose company names begin with a given letter (that the user must enter in a text box).

To test this example you must:

- create a form called **Clients**,
- add the following controls into this form:
  - a text box called **txtCieName**.
  - a list box called **lstCie**.
  - a command button called **cmdList1**.

Here is the example in VBA using an SQL SELECT query. The results of the SQL query provide the contents of the list.

```
Private Sub cmdList1_Click()
Dim strSQL As String

'    Checking the entered name
If txtCieName = "" Then
   MsgBox "You must enter at least one letter", vbExclamation
   txtCieName.SetFocus
   Exit Sub
End If

'    Properties of the drop-down list box
'    The list contains a query
Me.lstCie.RowSourceType = "Table/Query"
strSQL = "SELECT Clients.CLI_COMPANY FROM Clients " _
   & "WHERE (Clients.CLI_COMPANY Like '" & Me.txtCieName & "*')"
Me.lstCie.RowSource = strSQL

'    Refreshing the data in the list
Me.lstCie.Requery

End Sub
```

Here is an equivalent example in VBA without an SQL query. A set of values provides the contents of the list.

```
Private Sub cmdList2_Click()
Dim cncInvoices As ADODB.Connection
Dim rstClient As ADODB.Recordset
Dim strCieName as String

'   Checking the entered name
If txtCieName = "" Or IsNull(txtCieName) Then
   MsgBox "You must enter at least one letter", vbExclamation
   txtCieName.SetFocus
   Exit Sub
End If

'   Initializing the drop-down list
'   The list contains a set of values
Me.lstCie.RowSourceType = "Set of values"
Me.lstCie.RowSource = ""
Me.lstCie.Requery

'   Opening a Recordset
Set cncInvoices = CurrentProject.Connection
Set rstClient = New ADODB.Recordset
rstClient.Open "CLIENTS", cncInvoices, adOpenForwardOnly, _
adLockOptimistic

'   Running through the table and adding elements to the list
Do While Not rstClient.EOF
   If Left(rstClient("CLI_COMPANY"), 1) = Left(Me.txtCieName, _
   Len(Me.txtCieName)) Then
      strCieName = rstClient("CLI_COMPANY")
      Me.lstCie.AddItem strCieName
   End If
                                                                .../...
```

```
.../...
    rstClient.MoveNext
Loop
rstClient.close

End Sub
```

The examples above demonstrate that using SQL produces shorter VBA code that runs faster, especially if the tables concerned contain many records.

Chapter 6: Managing events

A. Introduction

1. What is an event?

An **event** is the action of the user or the system on an object. The event triggers the corresponding event procedure of the activated object.

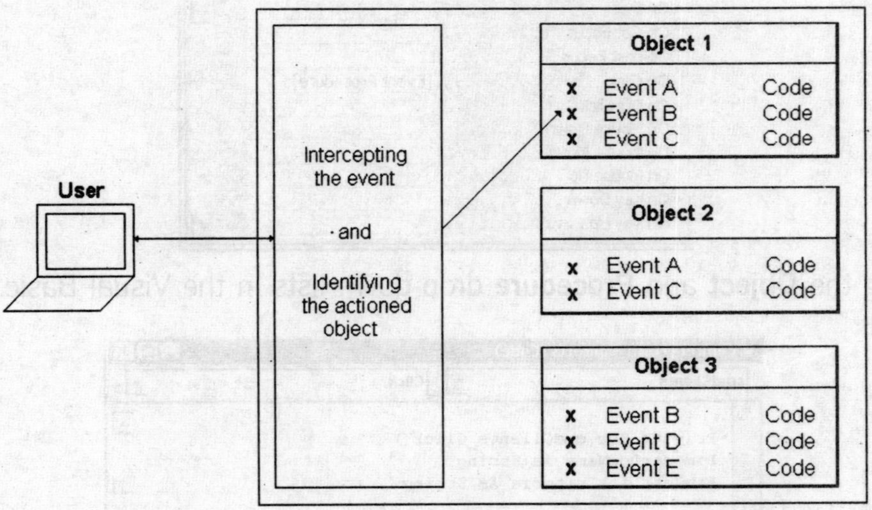

Defining an event procedure or a macro allows you to specify the application's response to an event that occurs in a form, a report or a control.

2. Associating VBA code with an event

You can assign VBA code to the object event in two ways:

– using the **Event** page of the object's properties in Access.

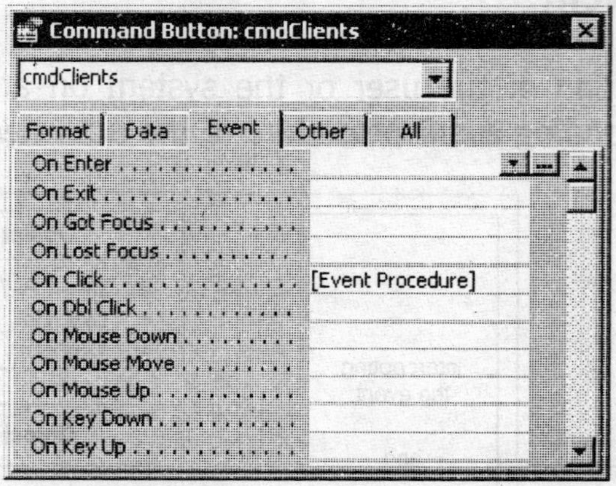

– using the **Object** and **Procedure** drop-down lists in the Visual Basic editor.

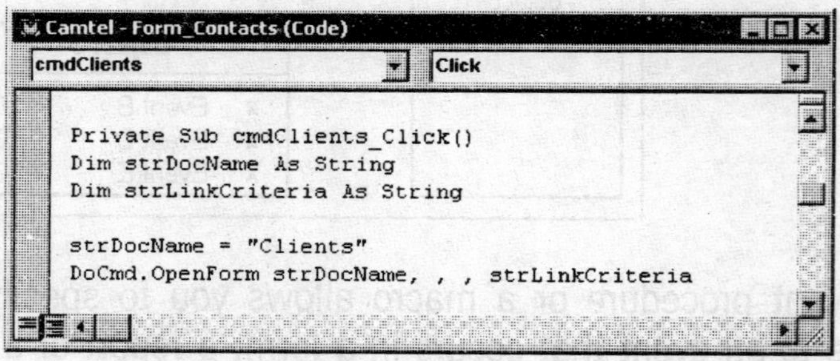

B. Event categories

This section lists events according to their type and action. It shows the following information for each event:

- name of the event,
- name of the corresponding property in the object's property window (this name appears between brackets),
- description of the event,
- whether or not you can cancel the event (this indication appears in the right-hand column, under **Cancel**). Section C of this chapter discusses canceling events.

1. Window events

		Cancel
Open	(On Open) occurs when a form opens, before it displays the first record, or when a report opens, before it is printed.	Yes
Load	(On Load) occurs after a form opens, when it displays the first record.	No
Resize	(On Resize) occurs when a form appears for the first time and when it is resized.	No
UnLoad	(On Unload) occurs as a form closes: when it unloads the records, before the form disappears.	Yes

Close	(On Close) occurs when a form closes and disappears.	No

2. Focus events

You can apply focus events to forms (Activate, Deactivate, GotFocus and LostFocus) or to controls (Enter, Exit, GotFocus and LostFocus).

An object is said to have the focus when it can receive user entries via the mouse or the keyboard. Objects that have the focus are called active objects (ActiveForm or ActiveControl).

The **SetFocus** method moves the focus to a form or to a control.

		Cancel
Activate	(On Activate) occurs when a window or a form becomes active.	No
Deactivate	(On Deactivate) occurs when you close a window, or when you activate another window, but before the new window becomes active.	No
Enter	(On Enter) occurs when you open a form, or when you move the focus from one control to another, but before the new control receives the focus.	No

Exit	(On Exit) occurs when you move the focus from one control to another, in the same or in another form, but before the old control loses the focus.	Yes
GotFocus	(On GotFocus) occurs when a control receives the focus, or when a form without an active control receives the focus.	No
LostFocus	(On LostFocus) occurs when a control or a form loses the focus.	No

3. Data events

Data events apply to forms that are associated with data sources (in this case the **RecordSource** property contains the name of a table or query) or to controls that are associated with a field of the form's data source (in this case the **ControlSource** property contains a value).

		Cancel
AfterInsert	(After Insert) occurs when you add a new record to a table.	No
AfterUpdate	(After Update) occurs when you update a control or a record.	No

AfterDelConfirm	(After Del Confirm) occurs when you confirm that you want to delete records.	No
BeforeInsert	(Before Insert) occurs when you enter the first character of a new record but before the record is added.	Yes
BeforeUpdate	(Before Update) occurs before you update a control or a modified record.	Yes
BeforeDelConfirm	(Before Del Confirm) occurs after you indicate that you want to delete records but before you confirm the deletion.	Yes
NotInList	(On Not in List) occurs when you enter a value in a combo box that is not in the combo box's list and the **Limit to List** property is set to Yes.	No
Current	(On Current) occurs when the focus moves from one record to another, or on opening, before the first record becomes current.	No
Change	(On Change) occurs on modification of a text or combo box (from the keyboard or by macro/VBA).	No

Updated	(On Updated) occurs when the data of an OLE object are modified.	No
Delete	(On Delete) occurs just before deletion (when you press the Del button, for example).	Yes
Dirty	(On Dirty) occurs on modification of a form or the text part of a combo box, or when you move from one page to another in a Tab control.	Yes

4. Mouse events

		Cancel
Click	(On Click) occurs when you click a control or another object in a form.	No
DblClick	(On Dbl Click) occurs when you double-click a control or another object in a form.	Yes
MouseDown	(On Mouse Down) occurs when you press a mouse button.	Yes
MouseMove	(On Mouse Move) occurs when you move the mouse.	No

MouseUp	(On Mouse Up) occurs when you release a mouse button.	No

5. Keyboard events

		Cancel
KeyDown	(On Key Down) occurs when you press a key or when you run a **SendKeys** statement or macro action. However, you can prevent the object from receiving the event by assigning a zero value to the **Keycode** argument of the object's **KeyDown** procedure.	No
KeyPress	(On Key Press) occurs when you press a key that sends a standard ANSI character or when you run a **SendKeys** statement or macro action. However, you can prevent the object from receiving the event by assigning a zero value to the **KeyAscii** argument of the object's **KeyPress** procedure.	Yes (by macro or VBA)
ImKeyUp	(On Key Up) occurs when you release a key or when you run a **SendKeys** statement or macro action. However, you can prevent the object from receiving the event by assigning a zero value to the **Keycode** argument of the object's **KeyUp** procedure.	No

The **KeyPreview** property of a form determines whether or not form-level keyboard event procedures will be called before control-level keyboard event procedures. You can use the **KeyPreview** property to create a form-level keyboard event management procedure.

Example

This example displays a form when the user presses the F1 key, whatever the active control.

```
Private Sub Form_Load()
KeyPreview = True
End Sub

Private Sub Form_KeyDown(KeyCode As Integer, Shift As Integer)
' Displays the search form when the F1 key is pressed
' Resets KeyCode, so as not to display the Access Help
If KeyCode = vbKeyF1 Then
    DoCmd.OpenForm "Search"
    KeyCode = 0
End If
End Sub
```

6. Print events

These events apply to Access reports.

		Cancel
Format	(On Format) occurs when Access determines which data belongs to which sections.	Yes

Print	(On Print) occurs when the data in a section has been formatted for printing.	Yes
Retreat	(On Retreat) occurs as Access returns to a previous section, when a report is being formatted.	No
NoData	(On No Data) occurs when Access has formatted for printing, a report that contains no data.	Yes
Page	(On Page) occurs when Access has formatted a report for printing, but before it is printed.	No

The Format, Print and Retreat events apply to report sections.

7. Filter events

		Cancel
ApplyFilter	(On Apply Filter) occurs when the user has applied a filter.	Yes
Filter	(On Filter) occurs when the user has created a filter.	Yes

8. Error and Timer events

		Cancel
Error	(On Error) occurs when an error occurs.	No
Timer	(On Timer) occurs when a specified time interval elapses.	No

C. Canceling an event

In some cases, it is better to cancel an event. You can do this in two ways:

- by specifying, as a parameter of the corresponding event property, the name of a macro that contains the **CancelEvent** action. For example, to cancel the update of a control, you can assign the name of the macro that contains the **CancelEvent** action, as a setting of the control's **Before Update** property. In VBA, the **CancelEvent** action uses the **CancelEvent** method of the **DoCmd** object.
- by assigning the value **True** to the **Cancel** argument of an event procedure.

Example

*This example cancels the **Exit** event if the date is incorrect: the cursor stays on the field.*

```
Private Sub txtEndDate_Exit(Cancel As Integer)

If IsNull(txtEndDate) Then Exit Sub

' The date must be valid
If Not IsDate(txtEndDate) Then
    MsgBox "Incorrect date", vbCritical
    Cancel = True
    Exit Sub
End If

' The end date must be >= the start date
If DateValue(txtEndDate) < DateValue(txtStartDate) Then
    MsgBox "The end date is earlier than the start date", _
    vbCritical
    Cancel = True
    Exit Sub
End If

End Sub
```

You cannot cancel all events (see the event categories list above).

D. Event sequences

A user or system action that triggers an event can also generate a sequence of underlying events.

Here are some examples of such event sequences:

Opening a form:

Open → Load → Resize → Activate → Current

Closing a form:

UnLoad → Deactivate → Close

Moving onto a control:

Enter → GotFocus

Leaving a control:

Exit → LostFocus

Moving from one form to another:

Deactivate (form1) → Activate (form2)

Modifying a text box:

KeyDown → KeyPress → Change → KeyUp

Updating a control:

KeyDown → KeyPress → Change → KeyUp → Exit (Area1) → LostFocus (Area1) → Enter (Area2) → GotFocus (Area 2)

Updating a record:

KeyDown → KeyPress → Change → KeyUp → BeforeUpdate (Text Box) → AfterUpdate (Text Box) → BeforeUpdate (Form) → AfterUpdate (Form)

Entering in the first field of a new record:

KeyDown → KeyPress → BeforeUpdate (Form) → Change → KeyUp

Deleting records:

Delete → Current → BeforeDelConfirm → AfterDelConfirm

E. Update events

Microsoft Access provides two types of update event:

- events that update controls,
- events that update records.

Updating a control runs the **BeforeUpdate** event and the **AfterUpdate** event of the control.

Updating a record runs the **BeforeUpdate** event and the **AfterUpdate** event of the form.

The events that update the controls run before the events that update the records.

Chapter 7: Debugging and managing errors

A. The different types of error

With VBA, four types of error can occur:

- syntax errors,
- compile errors,
- run-time errors,
- logical errors.

1. Syntax errors

The VBA editor can detect syntax errors automatically, as you are entering your code.

You can activate the automatic syntax check in the VBA window, by choosing the **Tools - Options** menu option, selecting the **Editor** tab and activating the **Auto Syntax Check** option.

Example

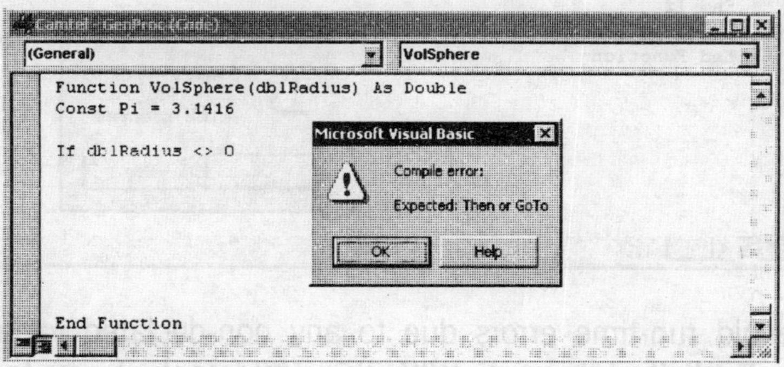

As this message indicates, syntax errors provoke compile errors.

2. Compile errors

VBA detects compile errors when it tries to compile your code.

You can compile your VBA code in two ways:

- on request, by selecting the **Debug - Compile** menu option; in this case Access will compile your code completely.
- automatically, **on execution of your code**; in this case Access will compile the contents of a procedure, on the first call to the procedure; Access will not compile any procedures that are not called.

It is advisable to compile your programs before you run them, as this approach will save software development time.

Example

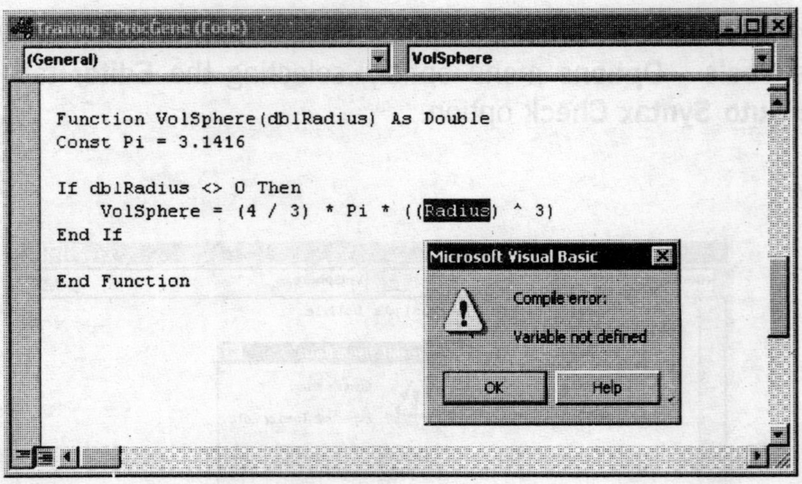

You can avoid run-time errors due to any non-declared variables by using the **Option Explicit** statement. With this statement, if you try to use a variable without declaring it, Access will raise an error at compile time.

3. Run-time errors

Access detects run-time errors when it tries to run your code. An invalid statement, operation or function call, etc. will provoke a run-time error. For example, you will generate a run-time error if you try to use a variable that contains a non-numeric value.

Example

In this example, a non-numeric value was transmitted to the VolSphere function as the dblRadius argument.

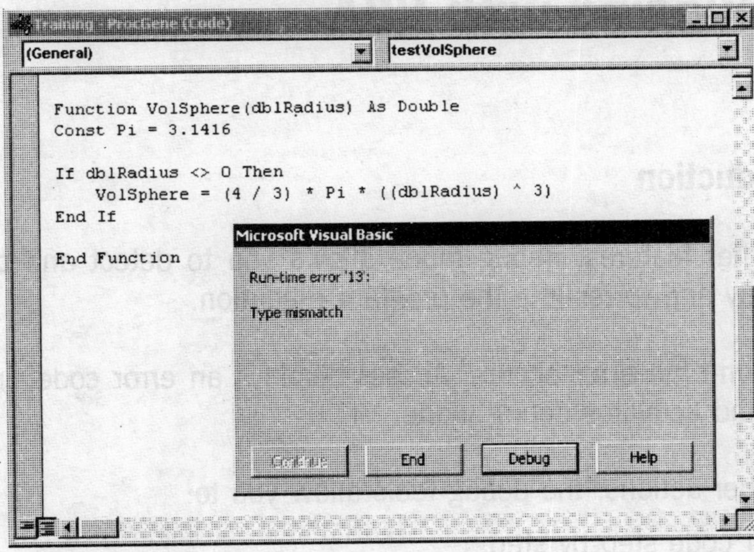

4. Logical errors

Logical errors are caused by mistakes in reasoning or by badly expressing correct reasoning in VBA code. For example, a calculation algorithm may produce a logical error if it contains a mistake or if one of its operations is omitted or badly expressed in VBA.

Logical errors are the most difficult ones to detect. They do not generally provoke run-time errors, but they do not produce the expected results either.

For instance, in the examples used above, **VolSphere** will not return the correct results if **Pi** has an inappropriate value or if the calculation formula is wrong.

B. Debugging with VBA

1. Introduction

Among other features, debug mode allows you to detect and correct errors interactively and to resume the program execution.

When a run-time error occurs, Access displays an error code, interrupts the program and activates debug mode.

Among other actions, the debug tools allow you to:

- run your code step by step,
- add breakpoints,
- view the value of a variable or an expression, at any time,
- modify your code interactively.

2. Debug toolbar

As its name suggests, the **Debug** toolbar provides the different debug tools.

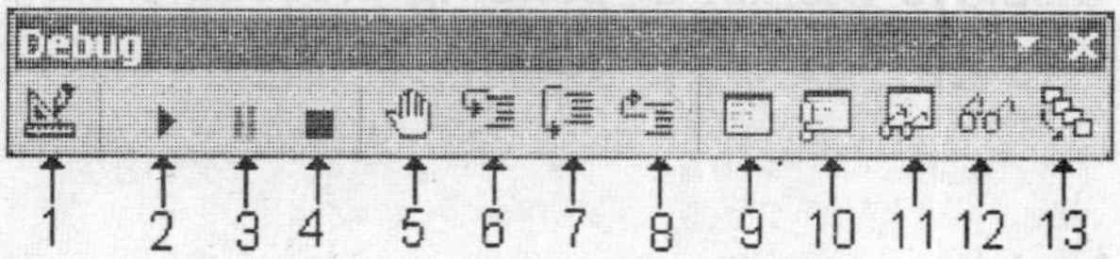

1. **Design Mode**: activates or deactivates Design Mode.

2. **Run** (F5): runs the current procedure, the active **UserForm** or a macro.

3. **Break** (Ctrl Pause): pauses the current program and goes into Break mode.

4. **Reset**: clears the contents of variables and resets the project.

5. **Toggle Breakpoint** (F9): defines or removes a breakpoint on the current line; the program runs until the breakpoint and goes into debug mode.

6. **Step Into** (F8): steps through the current procedure and any called procedures.

7. **Step Over** (Shift F8): steps through only the current procedure (running any called procedures as units).

8. **Step Out** (Ctrl Shift F8): runs the rest of the current procedure.

9. **Locals Window**: displays the values of the procedure's local variables.

10. **Immediate Window** (Ctrl G): displays the **Immediate** window to allow you to run statements interactively.

11. **Watch Window**: displays the list of watch expressions.

12. **Quick Watch** (Shift F9): displays the current value of the selected expression.

13. **Call Stack**: displays the list of pending procedure calls.

3. Debug object

The **Debug** object transmits data to the **Immediate** window at run-time.

Methods

Print

displays text or the result of an expression in the **Immediate** window.

Assert

pauses execution conditionally at the line that contains the method.

Example

```
VolSphere = (4 / 3) * Pi * ((dblRadius) ^ 3)
Debug.Print dblRadius
Debug.Assert VolSphere > 0
```

C. Handling errors with VBA

1. Introduction

When a run-time error occurs, Access generates an error code. To handle the error you can identify it by intercepting its code then deal with the error, for example by:

- displaying a more explicit message than that provided by the system,
- possibly correcting the error.

According to where the error occurs, Access' error handling system allows you to intercept the error in one of two ways:

- in the **Error** event procedure of a form or a report, if the error occurs at Access interface level or at Microsoft Jet engine level,
- using the **On Error** statement, if the error occurs in the VBA code.

To deal with errors, you need to interpret the error codes. Appendix A contains a list of error codes.

2. Error event procedure

The **Error** event procedure uses two arguments:

```
Sub Form_Error (DataErr As Integer, Response As Integer)
```

`DataErr` contains the error code.

`Response` allows you to display (`acDataErrDisplay`) or not display (`acDataErrContinue`) the standard Access error message.

Example

This example intercepts an error and displays a specific message instead of the standard Access message number 3058 (Can't have Null value in index).

```
Sub Form_Error(DataErr As Integer, Response As Integer)
    If DataErr = 3058 Then
        'Index has a Null value
        MsgBox "Each employee must have a number"
        'Preventing display of the standard Access message
        Response = acDataErrContinue
    End If
End Sub
```

3. On Error statement

➔ On Error GoTo

The **On Error GoTo** statement indicates a routine that must run in the case of an error. You must include this statement before any statements that are liable to provoke an error.

Syntax

```
On Error {GoTo <label> | GoTo 0}
```

`<label>` is the name of the label that marks the beginning of the error handling routine; a label consists of a name (which must start by a letter) followed by a colon (:).
It is generally advisable to place the error-handling statements after an **Exit Sub** or **Exit Function** statement in order to ensure that they will not run if an error does not occur.

deactivates the error handling.

In addition, the error handling routine must indicate where the procedure or function must resume execution after the error handling. For this purpose, you must use one of the following statements:

`Resume` continues program execution at the statement that provoked the error.

`Resume Next` continues program execution at the statement following that which provoked the error.

`Resume <label>` continues program execution at the specified label.

Example

```
Sub MyProcedure()
    On Error GoTo ErrorLabel
    ...
    Exit Sub
    ErrorLabel:
    Select Case Err
                                                    .../...
```

```
.../...
    Case 11
        ' Division by zero
        MsgBox ...
        ...
        Resume Next
    Case 13
        ' Type mismatch
        ...
    End Select
End Sub
```

4. Err object

The **Err** object contains information that helps you to identify the cause of an error.

Properties

Description returns a string explaining the cause of the error.

HelpContext returns the context ID for the Help file topic.

HelpFile returns a string containing the fully qualified path to the Help file.

LastDLLError returns a system error code that a call to a DLL (*Dynamic Link Library*) generates.

Number returns the error number.

Source returns a string containing the name of the object or application that generated the error.

Methods

Clear explicitly clears the contents of the **Err** object.

Raise allows you to generate run-time errors.

Example

This example displays information on an error.

```
Sub MyProcedure()
    On Error GoTo ErrorLabel
    ...
    Exit Sub

ErrorLabel:
    MsgBox "An error has occurred: " & vbCrLf & vbCrLf _
    & "Error N° " & Err.Number & ": " & Err.Description _
    & vbCrLf & vbCrLf _
    & "During execution of the application: " & Err.Source
End Sub
```

Here is an example of the message box that appears when an error occurs:

Chapter 8: Customizing forms and reports

A. Introduction

The VBA language allows you to customize your forms and reports. For example, you can carry out the following modifications:

- change the appearance of a control in a form or a report (by changing its color, size, position and so forth).
- add or delete controls in the form or report.
- link forms together using command buttons.
- display or print a report.
- apply filters to the records of a form or a report.

The **Command Button Wizard** and the **Combo Box Wizard** generate code automatically in event procedures. They help you to customize your forms and reports.

The mini-application in Chapter 13 describes other ways of customizing forms and reports.

B. Customizing forms

An open **Form** object belongs to the **Forms** collection, which represents all the forms that are currently open. The **ActiveForm** (**Screen.ActiveForm**) object and the **Me** object refer to the current form.

Use the **Me** keyword to refer to a **Form** or **Report** object, only in your class module code. In a standard or other type of form or report module you should specify the full reference of the **Form** or **Report** object.

1. Syntax

You can **refer to a form** as an object in a collection in a number of ways:

```
Forms!<FormName>
   for example: Forms!Orders
Forms![<FormName>]
   for example: Forms![Orders]
Forms("<FormName>")
   for example: Forms("Orders")
Forms(<Index>)
   for example: Forms(0)
```

The `Forms![<FormName>]` syntax is the most commonly used.

If the form name contains a space, the **Forms!FormName** syntax does not work. Always use the same syntax throughout your application, to make your code more readable and easier to maintain. It is better to refer to a specific form by its name rather than by its index, as its index can change.

To **refer to a subform** from a form, you must use the name of the control that contains the subform followed by a dot followed by the **Form** keyword.

Examples

```
[sFrmParticipant].Form!txtTraineeNbr
[sFrmTrainingPrograms].Form.RecordSource = strSQL
[sFrmTrainingPrograms].Form.Requery
```

2. Properties of the Form object

An asterisk (*) denotes a new property introduced by Access 2002 VBA. The following properties are not available in Design View.

AllowDataSheetView* indicates whether or not you can display the form in Datasheet View.

AllowFormView* indicates whether or not you can display the form in Form View.

AllowPivotChartView* indicates whether or not you can display the form in PivotChart View.

AllowPivotTableView* indicates whether or not you can display the form in PivotTable View.

Application allows you to access the Microsoft Access **Application** object.

BatchUpdates* indicates whether or not the form supports transacted batch updates.

BookMark defines a bookmark that uniquely identifies a record.

ChartSpace* returns a **ChartSpace** object.

CommitOnClose* indicates whether or not the specified form saves its modified records to the database when you close the form.

CommitOnNavigation* indicates whether or not the specified form saves its modified records to the database when you navigate from one record to another.

CurrentRecord identifies the current record.

CurrentSectionLeft determines the distance in twips between the left edge of the current section and the left edge of the form.

CurrentSectionTop determines the distance in twips between the top edge of the current section and the top edge of the form.

CurrentView returns the current view of the specified form.

DatasheetBackColor determines the background color of the whole table, query or form in Datasheet view.

DatasheetBorderLineStyle* indicates the line style that the datasheet border uses.

DatasheetCellEffects specifies if special effects are applied to cells in a datasheet.

DatasheetColumn HeaderUnderlineStyle* indicates the line style you must use for the lower edge of the column headers on the datasheet.

DatasheetFontHeight	indicates the font height in points you must use to display or print field names and data in Datasheet view.
DatasheetFontItalic	puts the field names and data in Datasheet view into italics.
DatasheetFontName	indicates the font used to display or print field names and data in Datasheet view.
DatasheetFontUnderline	underlines field names and data in Datasheet view.
DatasheetFontWeight	indicates the line width of the font used to display or print field names and data in Datasheet view.
DatasheetForeColor	determines the color of all the text in a table, query or form in Datasheet view.
DatasheetGridlinesBehavior	determines the type of gridlines to be used in a datasheet.
DatasheetGridlinesColor	determines the color of the gridlines in a datasheet.
Dirty	indicates whether or not the current record has been changed since it was last saved.
Form	refers to the form associated with a subform control.

Hwnd	returns the handle (a unique Long Integer value) assigned to the current window by Microsoft Windows.
HorizontalDataSheetGridlineStyle*	indicates the horizontal gridlines used on the datasheet.
InsideHeight	determines the height in twips of the window that contains the form.
InsideWidth	determines the width in twips of the window that contains the form.
Module	specifies a form module.
Moveable*	indicates whether or not the user can move the form.
NewRecord	determines whether or not the current record is a new record.
OpenArgs	returns the string expression specified by the **OpenArgs** argument of the **OpenForm** method that opened the form.
Page	specifies the current page number.
Pages	indicates the total number of pages.
Painting	indicates whether or not the form is repainted.
PaintPalette	specifies the palette that the form must use.

Parent	refers to the parent object.
PictureData	copies a picture from the form into another object that supports the **Picture** property.
PivotTable*	returns a **PivotTable** object that contains a PivotTable view on the form.
Printer*	returns or defines the **Printer** object that represents the default printer of the current system.
PrtDevMode	returns or defines information concerning the printing device mode for the form.
PrtDevNames	returns or defines information concerning the selected printer.
PrtMip	returns or defines information concerning the printing device mode for the specified device.
RecordsetClone	refers to the **Recordset** of the form.
Recordset	returns or defines the DAO **Recordset** object that represents the record source for the form.
RecordSourceQualifier*	returns or defines a string that indicates the owner of the SQL Server record source for the form.

Section	identifies a section that allows you to access the properties of a section of the form.
SelHeight	specifies or determines the number of rows (records) selected in the current selection rectangle.
SelLeft	specifies or determines the leftmost column (field) in the selection rectangle.
SelTop	specifies or determines the uppermost row (record) in the selection rectangle.
SelWidth	specifies or determines the number of columns (fields) selected in the current selection rectangle.
UseDefaultPrinter*	indicates whether or not the form uses the default system printer.
VerticalDatasheetGridlineStyle*	indicates the vertical gridline style used in the datasheet.
WindowHeight	indicates the height of the form in twips.
WindowLeft*	indicates, in twips the screen position of the left edge of the form.
WindowTop*	indicates, in twips the screen position of the top edge of the form.
WindowWidth	indicates the width of the form in twips.

3. Methods of the Form object

An asterisk (*) denotes a new method introduced by Access 2002 VBA.

GotoPage moves the focus to the first control on the indicated page.

Move* moves or resizes the form to the coordinates indicated by the argument values.

Recalc immediately recalculates all the form controls.

Refresh updates the form's data in line with changes that you and other users have made.

Repaint completes any pending updates for the form.

Requery updates the data underlying the specified form.

SetFocus gives the focus to the form.

UnDo resets the form to its state before modification.

Examples

The following example displays the Client record that corresponds to the company name selected from a list.

```
Private Sub lstCliSearch_AfterUpdate()
Dim rs As Object

' Finding the record for the selected client
Set rs = Me.Recordset.Clone
rs.FindFirst "[Cli_CliCode] = '" & Me![lstCliSearch] & "'"
If Not rs.EOF Then Me.Bookmark = rs.Bookmark

End Sub
```

The following example assigns a filter according to the contents of a check box: for UK clients, foreign clients or all clients.

```
Private Sub chkCountry_AfterUpdate()

Select Case chkCountry
    ' UK clients
    Case 1
        Me.Filter = "[Cli_Country] = 'UK'"
        Me.FilterOn = True
    ' Foreign clients
    Case 2
        Me.Filter = "[Cli_Country] <> 'UK'"
        Me.FilterOn = True
                                              .../...
```

```
.../...
    ' All clients
    Case 3
        Me.FilterOn = False
End Select

End Sub
```

C. Customizing reports

An open **Report** object belongs to the **Reports** collection, which represents all the reports that are currently open. The **ActiveReport** (**Screen.ActiveReport**) object and the **Me** object refer to the current report.

1. Syntax

You can **refer to a report** as an object of a collection as you would refer to a form:

```
Reports![OrdList]
Reports!("OrdList")
Reports![OrdList]![OrdDate]
```

2. Properties not available in Design View

Property	Description
Application	allows you to access the Microsoft Access **Application** object.
CurrentRecord	identifies the current record.
CurrentX	specifies the horizontal coordinate for the starting position of the next printing or drawing method on a report.
CurrentY	specifies the vertical coordinate for the starting position of the next printing or drawing method on a report.
Dirty	determines whether or not the current record has been changed since it was saved last.
DrawMode	specifies how the pen (the color used for the drawing) interacts with the background colors on the report when you use the **Line**, **Circle** or **Pset** method to print lines on a report.
DrawStyle	specifies the line style when you use the **Line** or **Circle** method to print lines on a report.
DrawWidth	specifies the line width when you use the **Line** or **Circle** method to print lines on a report.
FillColor	specifies the fill color for rectangles and circles drawn on a report using the **Line** and **Circle** methods.
FillStyle	specifies whether a circle or a line drawn on a report using the **Line** or **Circle** method is transparent, opaque or filled with a pattern.

FontBold	specifies whether or not a font must appear in bold when you use the **Print** method to print report controls.
FormatCount	determines how many times the **OnFormat** property has been used for the current section of the report.
GroupLevel	refers to the group level you are using to group or sort in a report.
HasData	indicates whether or not the report is bound to an empty recordset.
Hwnd	returns the handle (a unique Long Integer value) assigned to the current window by Microsoft Windows.
Left	defines an object's leftmost position on the report.
Module	specifies a report module.
Moveable*	indicates whether or not the user can move the report.
MoveLayout	specifies whether or not Microsoft Access must move to the next printing position on the page.
NextRecord	specifies if a section must move to the next record.
Page	specifies the current page number.
Pages	indicates the total number of pages.
Painting	indicates whether or not the report is repainted.

PaintPalette	specifies the palette that the report must use.
Parent	refers to the parent object.
PictureData	copies a picture from the report into another object that rapports the **Picture** property.
PrintCount	indicates the number of times the **OnPrint** property has been calculated for the current section of a report.
Printer*	returns or defines the **Printer** object that represents the default printer of the current system.
PrintSection	specifies whether or not a section must be printed.
PrtDevMode	returns or defines information concerning the printing device mode for the report.
PrtDevNames	returns or defines information concerning the selected printer.
PrtMip	returns or defines information concerning the printing device mode for the specified device.
RecordSource Qualifier*	returns or defines a string that indicates the owner of the SQL Server record source for the report.
Report	refers to the report associated with a subreport control.
ScaleHeight	specifies the number of units in the height of the page when you use the **Line**, **Circle**, **Pset** or **Print** method to preview or print a report or to save it as a file.

ScaleLeft	specifies the number of units for the horizontal coordinates of the left edge of the page when you use the **Line**, **Circle**, **Pset** or **Print** method to preview or print a report or to save it as a file.
ScaleMode	specifies the measurement units coordinates on the page when you use the **Line**, **Circle**, **Pset** or **Print** method to preview or print a report or to save it as a file.
ScaleTop	specifies the number of units for the vertical coordinates of the top edge of the page when you use the **Line**, **Circle**, **Pset** or **Print** method to preview or print a report or to save it as a file.
ScaleWidth	specifies the number of units in the width of the page when you use the **Line**, **Circle**, **Pset** or **Print** method to preview or print a report or to save it as a file.
Section	identifies a section that allows you to access the properties of a section of the report.
Shape*	returns a string containing the **Shape** command that sorts or groups the specified report (this property is read-only).
Top	defines the uppermost position of an object on the report.
UseDefaultPrinter*	indicates whether or not the report uses the default system printer.
WindowLeft*	indicates, in twips, the screen position of the left edge of the report.

WindowTop* indicates, in twips, the screen position of the top edge of the report.

3. Methods

Circle draws a circle or an oval.

Line draws a line or a rectangle.

Move* moves or resizes the report to the coordinates indicated by the argument values.

Print returns the text defined for the **Report** object.

Pset defines the color of a point on the report.

Scale specifies the coordinates system for a **Report** object.

TextHeight gives the height of a text string.

TextWidth gives the width of a text string.

D.Control objects

A **Control** object belongs to the **Controls** collection, which represents all the controls on a form, a subform or a report. The **ActiveControl** (**Screen.ActiveControl** or **<FormName>.ActiveControl**) object refers to the active control.

1. Syntax

You can refer to a control either implicitly:

```
<Forms>|<Report>!<ControlName>        e.g.: Me!OrdDate
<Forms>|<Report>![<ControlName>]      e.g.: Me![OrdDate]
<Forms>|<Report>("<ControlName>")     e.g.: Me!("OrdDate")
<Forms>|<Report>.<ControlName>        e.g.: Me.OrdDate
```

or explicitly, as a member of the **Controls** collection:

```
<Form>|<Report>.Controls{("<control>")|!<control>|
<control index>)}
For example:
  Me.Controls!OrdDate
  Me.Controls![OrdDate]
  Me.Controls("OrdDate")
  Me.Controls(0)
```

Each control has its own properties, methods and events. This section lists only the properties and methods that are common to most controls.

➲ To refer to the active form or report, you do not have to use the **Me** keyword: you can use the name of the control directly.

---

2. Properties common to most controls

Application allows you to access the Microsoft Access **Application** object.

Form refers to the form that contains the control.

Hyperlink refers to a hyperlink.

Object refers to an ActiveX object associated with an OLE object linked or embedded in a control.

ObjectVerbs indicates the list of OLE actions that the OLE object supports.

OldValue returns the unedited value of a bound control.

Parent refers to the parent object of a control.

Report refers to the report that contains the control.

3. Methods common to most controls

Requery recalculates the value of a control.

SetFocus gives the focus to a control.

SizeToFit adjusts a control to fit the text or image that it contains.

UnDo resets the control to its state before modification.

4. New Access 2002 method

Most controls provide the **Move** method (for example, **CheckBox**, **ComboBox**, **CommandButton**, **Image**, **Label**, **Line**, and **TextBox**).

The **Move** method allows you to move and/or resize the control according to the coordinates that the argument values indicate.

Syntax

```
<expression>.Move(<Left>, <Top>, <Width>, <Height>)
```

`expression`	refers to a control, a form or a report.
`Left`	(required) gives, in twips, the position on the screen of the left edge of the object with respect to the left edge of the Microsoft Access window.
`Top`	(optional) gives, in twips, the position on the screen of the top edge of the object with respect to the top edge of the Microsoft Access window.
`Width`	(optional) specifies the width of the object in twips.
`Height`	(optional) specifies the height of the object in twips.

E. Access controls

1. Introduction

Microsoft Access 2002 provides a number of useful controls that help you to develop your applications.

You can place these controls in your forms and reports to create the required interface. Each of these controls has its own properties, methods and list of events to which it can react. You can access these features from the **Object Browser**.

There are two types of control:

- **intrinsic** controls, which are integrated into the Access engine,
- **ActiveX** controls, each of which is contained in an OCX file.

The **Toolbox** provides the intrinsic controls.

You can select the ActiveX controls using the  button in the **Toolbox**. This tool button lists all the ActiveX controls that the system offers. ActiveX controls work like intrinsic controls. You include them in your system when you install new applications or ActiveX control libraries.

The Microsoft Office XP Professional edition provides the Calendar control, which helps you to display and update a calendar.

2. List of Access 2002 controls

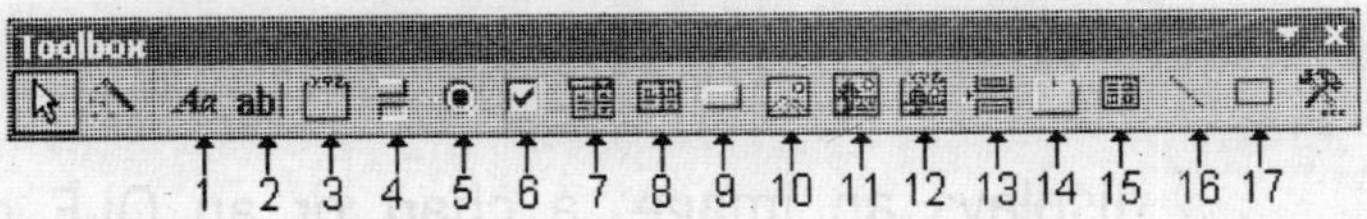

Label (1) — displays text.

Text Box (2) — allows you to enter text.

Option Group (3) — groups a set of options.

Toggle Button (4) — indicates if an option is activated or deactivated.

Option Button (5) — indicates if an option is activated or not.

Check Box (6) — indicates if an option is activated or not.

Combo Box (7) — displays a text box and a list of values to choose from.

List Box (8) — displays a list of values.

Command Button (9) — runs an action when you click it.

Image (10) — displays an image.

Unbound Object Frame (11) — displays an image, a chart or an OLE object that is not stored in an Access table.

Bound Object Frame (12) — displays an image, a chart or an OLE object that is stored in an Access table.

Page Break (13) — starts a new screen or printed page.

Tab Control (14) — displays several tabs, each of which can contain controls.

Subform/Subreport (15) — creates a form within a form or a report within a report.

Line (16) — draws a line.

Rectangle (17) — draws a rectangle.

Chapter 9: Customizing the user interface

A. Startup options

The Access 2002 startup options define the look and behavior of the application on startup.

To modify the startup options, select the **Tools - Startup** command.

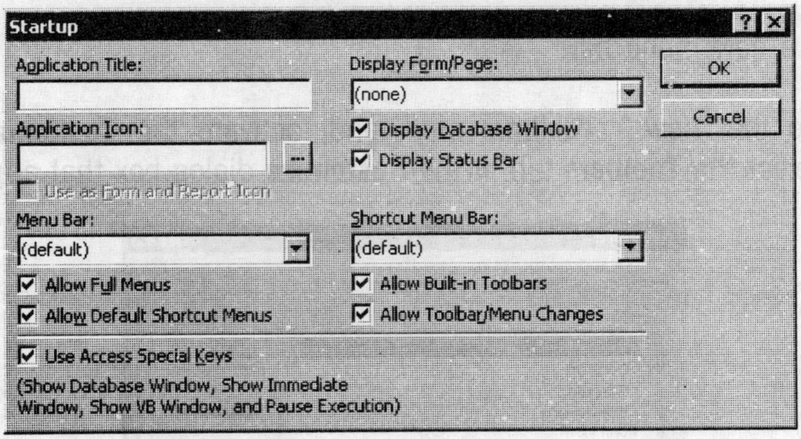

B. Managing menus

Microsoft Access 2002 manages menu bars, shortcut menus and toolbars with a common technology using the **CommandBar** object.

You can create command bars in two ways:

- via a graphic interface,
- by writing VBA code to handle the **CommandBar** object.

This section describes how to use the first of these methods to create a menu bar. The techniques for creating toolbars and shortcut menus are very similar to those for creating menu bars.

1. Creating a new menu bar

To create a new menu bar:

➔ Choose the **View - Toolbars** command, activate the **Customize** option and select the **Toolbars** tab in the **Customize** dialog box that appears.

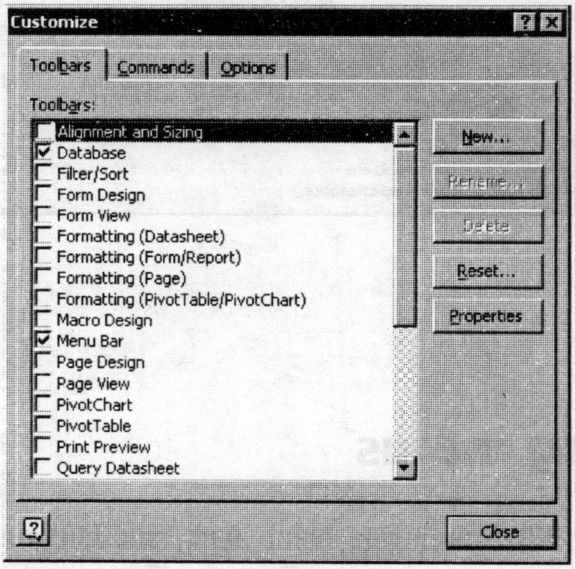

➔ Click the **New** button to add a new toolbar to the **Toolbars** list.

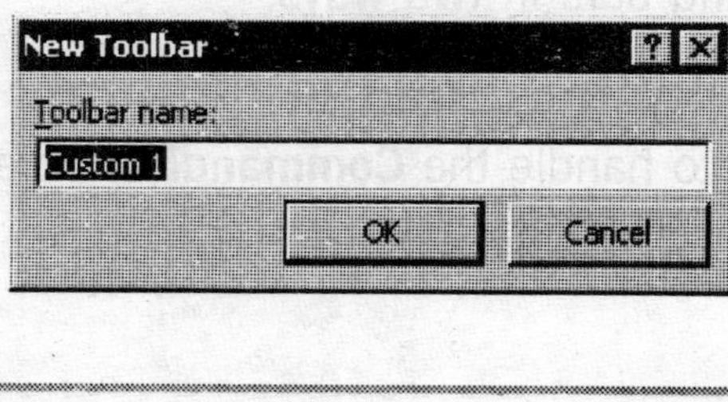

Change the **Toolbar name** (to DemoMenu, for example) and click **OK**.

➔ Click the **Properties** button and select the **Menu Bar** option from the **Type** drop-down list.

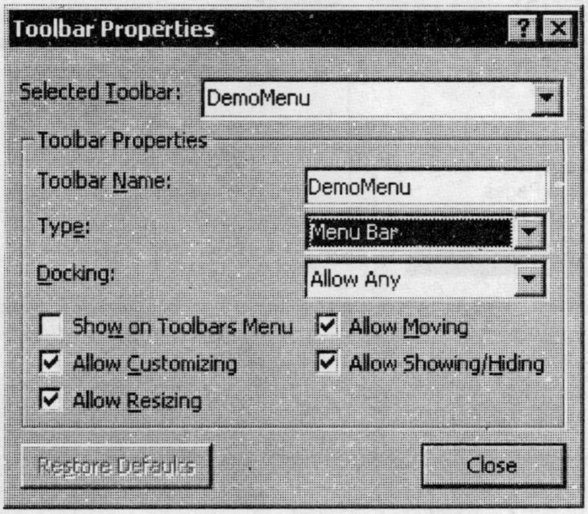

➔ Activate or deactivate any other of the options, as required.

2. Adding a menu to a menu bar

➔ Choose the **View - Toolbars - Customize** menu option.
Select your new menu bar (**DemoMenu**) in the **Toolbars** list.
Select the **Commands** tab.
In the **Categories** list, select **New Menu**.

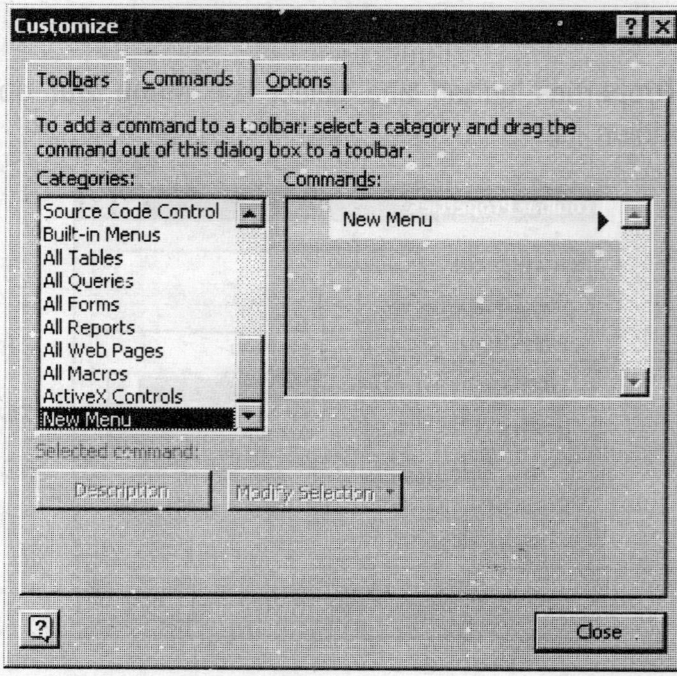

→ In the **Commands** frame, click **New Menu** and drag it onto the **DemoMenu** menu bar (which should have appeared on the screen when you selected it in the **Toolbars** list).

→ Customize your menu bar by changing its properties (right-click the **New Menu** button on the menu bar and choose **Properties**).

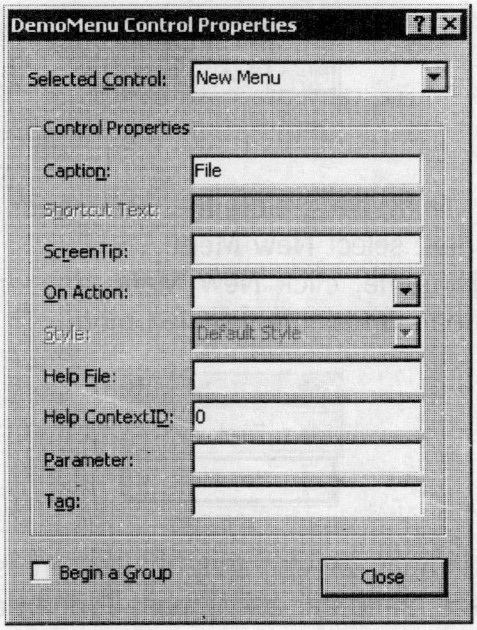

→ To add other menus to your menu bar, drag the **New Menu** option in the **Commands** frame of the **Customize** dialog box either to the left or to the right of one of the existing menus on the bar.

3. Adding a submenu to a menu

To add a submenu to a menu:

→ Choose the **View - Toolbars - Customize** option.
If necessary, select the menu bar in the **Toolbars** list (the menu bar appears on the screen).
Click the menu to which you want to add a submenu.

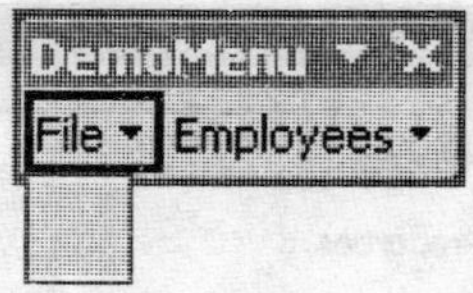

→ In the **Customize** dialog box, select the **Commands** tab.
In the **Categories** list, select **New Menu**.
In the **Commands** frame, click **New Menu** and drag it onto the empty area of the menu bar, under the selected menu.

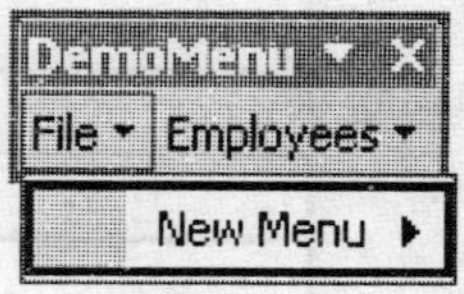

→ Customize this submenu by changing its properties (right-click the **New Menu** button on the menu bar and choose **Properties**).

→ To add other submenus to the menu, drag the **New Menu** option in the **Commands** frame of the **Customize** dialog box either above or below one of the existing submenus.

4. Adding commands

To add a command to a menu or to a submenu:

→ Choose the **View - Toolbars - Customize** option.
If necessary, select the menu bar in the **Toolbars** list (the menu bar appears on the screen).
Select the menu or the submenu to which you want to add a command.

→ In the **Customize** dialog box, select the **Commands** tab.
As required, select one of the **Categories** and drag one of the **Commands** onto the menu or submenu.

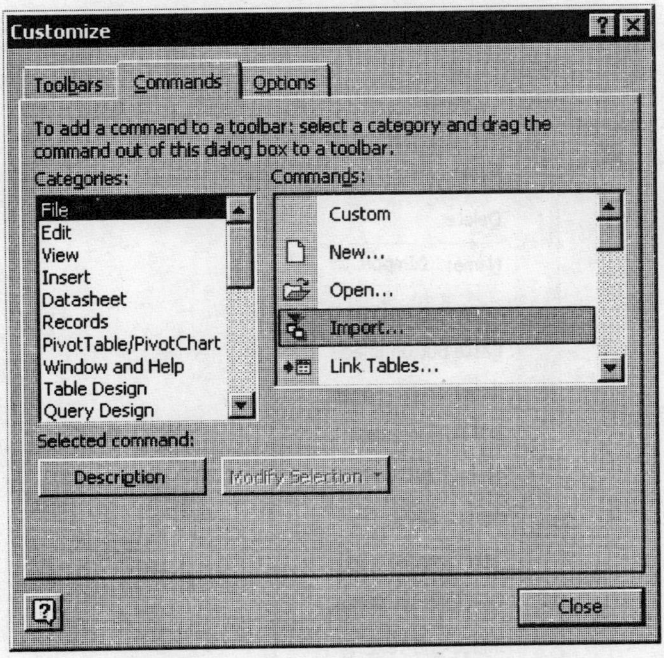

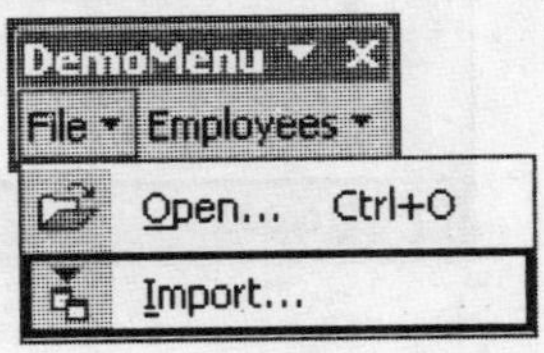

→ Right-click the command you have added, to open its shortcut menu.

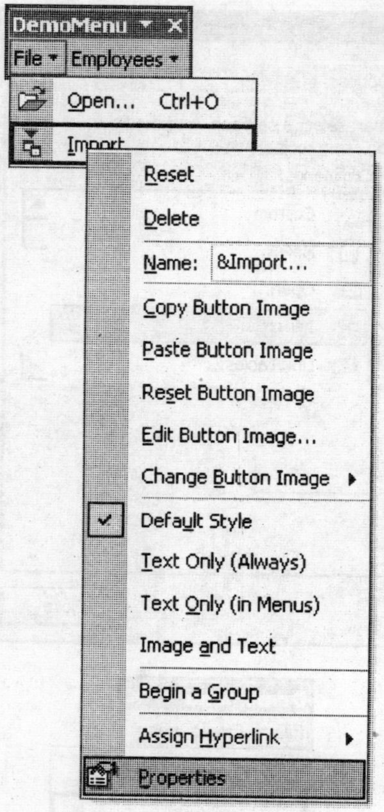

The shortcut menu for a command offers options to delete the command, to change the image associated with the command, to assign a hyperlink, to change the command's properties and so forth.

The **On Action** property allows you to specify the action that must run when you activate the command. You can either choose the name of a macro or enter the name of a Visual Basic function prefixed by an equals sign (either MacroName or =FunctionName()).

5. Using command bars

Using menu bars

You can associate a menu bar with a form or a report via the **Menu Bar** property of the form or report. You can associate a menu bar with the application by specifying the menu bar in the application's startup options (**Tools - Startup - Menu Bar** box).

Using shortcut menus

You can associate a shortcut menu with a form or a report via the **Shortcut Menu Bar** property of the form or report.

Using toolbars

If the application contains only one custom toolbar, use the **View - Toolbars** command to indicate that the toolbar must appear each time you start the application.

To associate a toolbar with a form or a report, use the **Toolbar** property of the form or report.

To display several custom toolbars, use the **Visible** property of the **CommandBar** object in the VBA code.

Chapter 10: Communicating with other Office XP applications

A. Automation technology

1. Introduction

Automation technology, also called **OLE** (*Object Linking and Embedding*) technology, allows you to handle objects from another application, directly in Access or VBA Access.

Automation requires a client and a server (called the **OLE server**). The server is the application or component that provides services to the client. The client (also called the **OLE controller**) uses these services to drive the application server and to handle its objects. For example, if you make a Word mail-shot from VBA Access, Access is the client and Word is the OLE server.

An **object library** is a file, generally with an .olb name extension, that provides information for handling the objects the server offers. You can use the **Object Browser** to view the contents of an object library.

Before you can access the objects of another application, you must activate its object library's reference, as follows:

➔ In the VBA window for a module, select the **Tools - References** command.

The **References** dialog box shows all the OLE servers in the registry database.

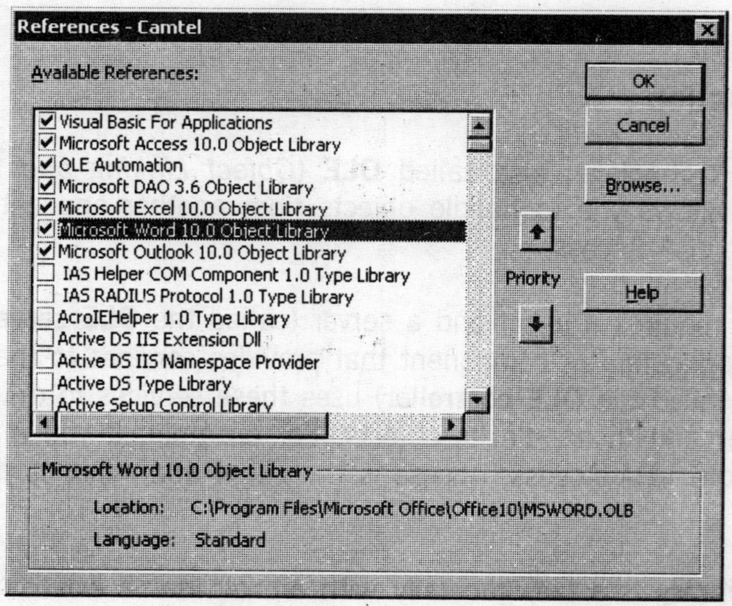

➜ Activate the required reference.

Use the **Object Browser** to view the list of objects, methods and properties of an OLE server.

2. Using Automation technology

To handle the objects of another application, carry out the following steps:

- define an object variable in the VBA code,
- use the **CreateObject** and **GetObject** functions to create and refer to the object.

Example

Starting Word:

```
Dim AppWord As Object
Set AppWord = CreateObject("Word.Application")
```

or

```
Dim appWord As New Word.Application
```

Referring to an existing Word document:

```
Dim DocWord As New Word.Document
Set DocWord = GetObject("C:\Clients\Chaseup.doc")
```

The following sections describe how you can use Automation technology to drive different applications in the Microsoft Office suite.

As the Microsoft Office suite offers large numbers of objects, collections, methods and properties, the following sections describe only those most commonly used.

B. Driving Word from Access

1. Word object model

Here is an extract from the Word object model:

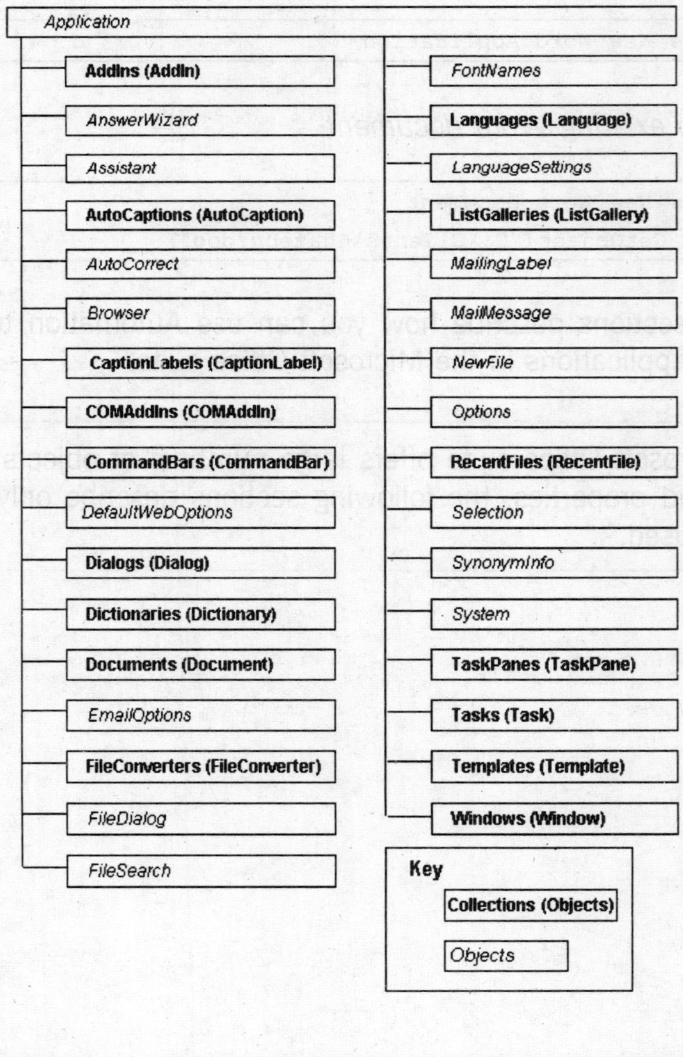

2. Word objects and collections

Documents this collection contains all the open **Document** objects.

Dictionaries this collection contains all the active custom **Dictionary** objects.

EmailOptions this object contains the global attributes that Microsoft Word uses when you create or change e-mail messages and responses.

FileConverters this collection contains all the **FileConverter** objects that are available for opening and saving files.

FontNames this object lists all the available fonts.

Languages this collection contains all the **Language** objects that Word uses for linguistic checks and formatting.

ListGalleries this collection of **ListGallery** objects represents the first three tabs in the **Bullets and Numbering** dialog box.

MaiMessage this object represents the active e-mail message if Word is your e-mail editor.

Options this object represents Word's application and document options. Most of the **Options** object's properties correspond to the items in the **Options** dialog box (which you can access from the **Tools** menu).

Selection this object represents the window or pane that is currently selected.

System this object contains information on your computer's system.

Templates this collection contains all the **Template** objects that are currently available.

3. Documents collection

The **Documents** collection contains all the **Document** objects that are open in Word.

Methods

Add creates a new document and adds it to the **Documents** collection; example: `Documents.Add Template:= "Normal"`

Close closes all open Word documents;
example: `Documents.Close`

Open opens the specified document and adds it to the **Documents** collection;
example:

```
Documents.Open
FileName:="C:\Clients\Chaseup.doc", _
ReadOnly:=True
```

Save saves all the open documents;
example: `Documents.Save`

4. Document object

A **Document** object refers to a Word document. As its name suggests, the **ActiveDocument** property refers to the active document.

Methods

Activate activates a document that is already open;
example: `Documents("Purchasing.doc").Activate`

Close closes an open Word document;
example: `Documents("Purchasing.doc").Close`
or `ActiveDocument.Close`

PrintPreview displays the print preview of a document;
example: `ActiveDocument.PrintPreview`

Range returns a **Range** object;
example: `ActiveDocument.Range(0, 50).Bold = _`
`True`

Save saves a document;
example: `ActiveDocument.Save`

SaveAs saves a document under a new name or format;
example: `ActiveDocument.SaveAs _`
`FileName:=strDocName`

Objects and collections

Characters is a collection of the characters in a document, a range or a selection.

MailMerge is a mail merge in Word.

PageSetup describes the formatting of a document; example: `ActiveDocument.PageSetup.RightMargin = InchesToPoints(1)`

Paragraphs is a collection of paragraphs in a document.

SmartTags is a collection of active **SmartTag** objects in a document or in a text range within a document.

Words is a collection of words in a document; example: `ActiveDocument.Words.Count`

Examples

This example puts the words of a document into bold style.

```
Private Sub Word_ToBold()
Dim appWord As New Word.Application

With appWord
    .Documents.Open "C:\Clients\Chaseup.doc"
    .ActiveDocument.Select
    .Selection.Font.Bold = True
    .ActiveDocument.Close wdSaveChanges
    .Quit
End With

End Sub
```

This example starts a mail merge.

```
Private Sub Mailshot()
Dim appWord As Word.Application
Dim docWord As Word.Document

' Starting Word
Set appWord = New Word.Application
appWord.Visible = True

' Opening the form letter
Set docWord = appWord.Documents.Open("C:\Clients\Chaseup.doc")

' Preparing a mail merge for all clients
With docWord.MailMerge
    .Destination = wdSendToNewDocument
    .SuppressBlankLines = True
    With .DataSource
        .FirstRecord = wdDefaultFirstRecord
        .LastRecord = wdDefaultLastRecord
    End With

' Starting the mail merge
    .Execute
End With

End Sub
```

C. Driving Excel from Access

1. Excel object model

Here is an extract from the Excel object model:

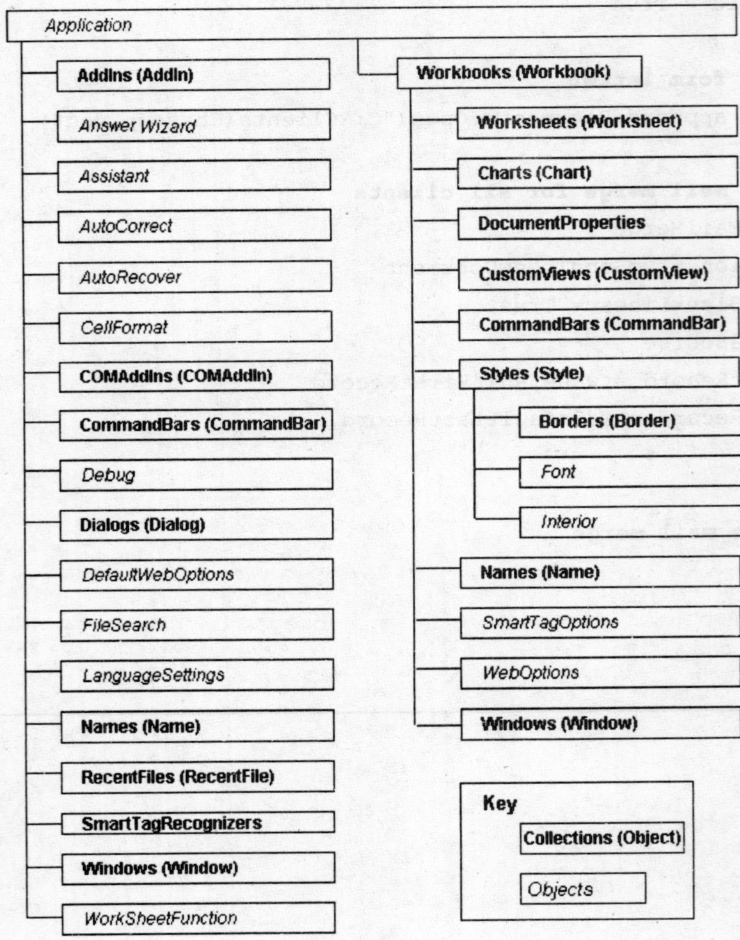

2. Excel objects and collections

Workbooks This collection contains all the open **Workbook** objects.

Worksheets This collection contains all the open **Worksheet** objects in a workbook.

Charts This collection contains all the **Chart** objects in a workbook.

Names This collection contains all the **Name** objects in the application or workbook. Each **Name** object identifies a range of cells.

SmartTag Options This object contains the **SmartTag** options that Microsoft Excel is using.
Example: activating the SmartTags:

```
ActiveWorkbook.SmartTagOptions _
.EmbedSmartTags = True
```

Styles This collection contains all the **Style** objects (style descriptions) in a workbook.

CustomViews This collection contains all the **CustomView** objects in a worksheet.

3. Workbooks collection

The **Workbooks** collection contains all the open **Workbook** objects.

Methods

Add creates a new workbook (which becomes the active workbook) and adds it to the **Workbooks** collection; example: `Workbooks.Add`

Close closes all open Excel workbooks; example: `Workbooks.Close`

Open opens the specified workbook (which becomes the active workbook) and adds it to the **Workbooks** collection; example:

```
Workbooks.Open _
FileName:="C:\Invoices\Invoices.xls"
```

Save saves all the open workbooks; example: `Workbooks.Save`

4. Workbook object

A **Workbook** object refers to an Excel workbook.

As its name suggests, the **ActiveWorkbook** property refers to the active workbook.

Methods

Activate activates a workbook that is already open;
example: `Workbooks("Purchasing.xls").Activate`

Close closes an open Excel workbook;
example: `Workbooks("Purchasing.xls").Close`
or `ActiveWorkbook.Close`

PrintPreview displays the print preview of the active worksheet in a workbook;
example: `ActiveWorkbook.PrintPreview`

Save saves a workbook
example: `ActiveWorkbook.Save`

SaveAs saves a workbook under a new name or format
example:
```
ActiveWorkbook.SaveAs FileName:= _
"Invoices.xlt"
```

5. Writing data to Excel cells

Example

This example displays the contents of an Access table in Excel.

```
Private Sub ExportXLS_Client()

' Access objects
Dim dbsInvoices As DAO.Database
Dim rstClient As DAO.Recordset
Dim fld As DAO.Field

' Excel objects
Dim appExcel As Excel.Application
Dim wkbClient As Excel.Workbook
Dim wksClient As Excel.Worksheet

' Loop variables
Dim intRow As Integer
Dim intCol As Integer

' Creating an Excel workbook
Set appExcel = CreateObject("Excel.Application")
Set wbkClient = appExcel.Workbooks.Add
Set wksClient = appExcel.ActiveSheet
appExcel.Visible = True

' Opening the Clients table
Set dbsInvoices = DBEngine.OpenDatabase("C:\Invoices\Invoices.mdb")
Set rstClient=dbsInvoices.OpenRecordset("Clients", dbOpenDynaset)
                                                          .../...
```

```
.../...
' Updating the active worksheet
With wksClient
' Setting column headers to field names
    intCol = 1
    For Each fld In rstClient.Fields
        .Cells(1, intCol).Value = fld.Name
        intCol = intCol + 1
    Next fld

' Scrolling through the records
' Adding one row per record
    intRow = 2
    Do While Not rstClient.EOF
        intCol = 1
        For Each fld In rstClient.Fields
            .Cells(intRow,intCol).Value = fld.Value
            intCol = intCol + 1
        Next fld
        intRow = intRow + 1
        rstClient.MoveNext
    Loop
    ' Assigning a name to an Excel worksheet
    .Name = "List of clients"

End With

' Saving the workbook
wkbClient.SaveAs "C:\Clients\Clients.xls"

' Closing Excel
appExcel.Quit

End Sub
```

D. Driving Outlook from Access

1. Outlook object model

Here is an extract from the Outlook object model:

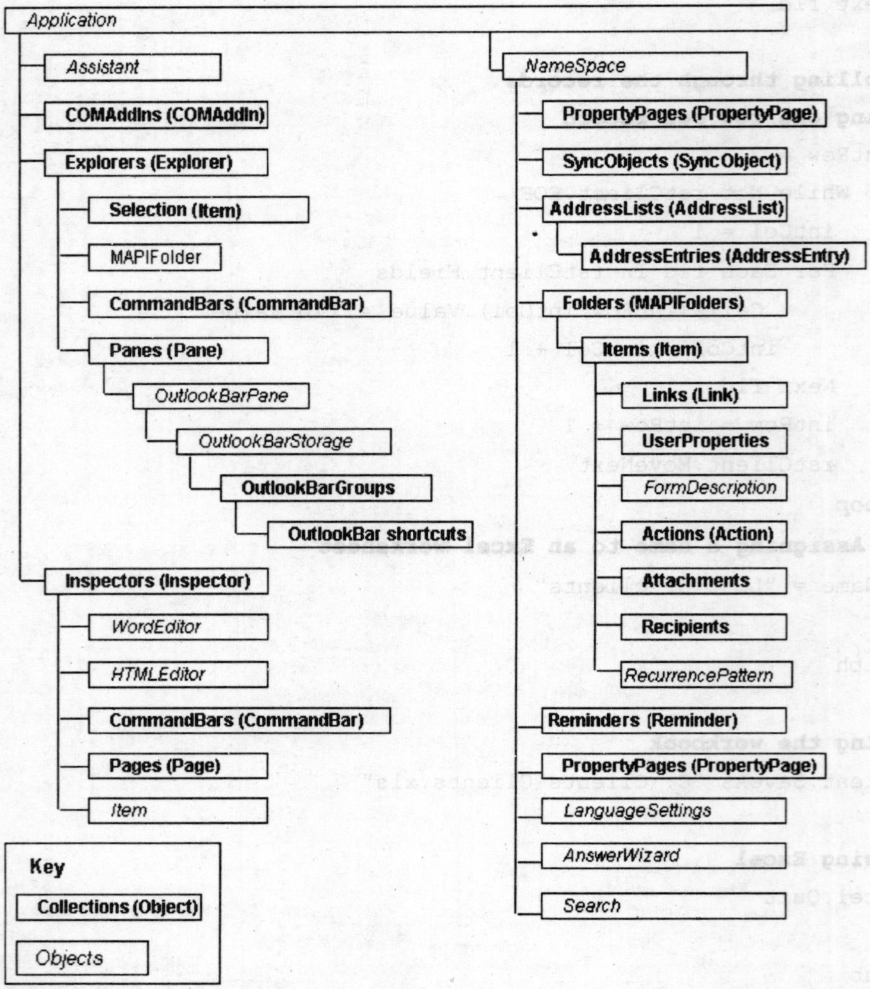

2. Example: displaying Outlook contacts

This example lists the names and e-mail addresses of Outlook contacts in a list box on an Access form.

To test this example, you must first carry out the following steps:

- create a new form,
- include a list box in the form called **lstContacts** and a command button called **cmdContacts**.

```
Private Sub lstContacts_Click()

Dim objOle As Outlook.Application
Dim objNamespace As NameSpace
Dim objAddrList As AddressList
Dim objAddrEntries As AddressEntries
Dim objAdrEntry As AddressEntry
Dim i As Integer

' Initialising the drop-down list
With Me.lstContacts
    .ColumnCount = 2
    .RowSourceType = "List of values"
End With

' Creating the object for the Outlook application
Set objOle = CreateObject("Outlook.Application")

' Opening the Contacts address list
Set objNamespace = objOle.GetNamespace("MAPI")
Set objAddrList = objNamespace.AddressLists("Contacts")
Set objAddrEntries = objAddrList.AddressEntries
```

.../...

```
.../...
' Accessing the first contact
Set objAdrEntry = objAddrEntries.GetFirst

' Adding contacts to the list
For i = 1 To objAddrEntries.Count
    With Me.lstContacts
        .AddItem objAdrEntry.Name
        .AddItem objAdrEntry.Address
    End With
'   Next contact
    Set objAdrEntry = objAddrEntries.GetNext
Next i

End Sub
```

E. DDE protocol

The DDE (*Dynamic Data Exchange*) protocol links together two Windows applications: one of the applications is called the **Destination** or **Client** application and the other is called the **Source** or **Server** application. The link is broken if one of these two applications closes.

The life-cycle of a DDE link is made up of three main phases:

- **initialization**: the destination application looks for and finds the source application and sets up a communications link (a channel).
- **conversation**: the two applications exchange data across the channel.
- **termination**: the channel is shut down.

1. Initialization

➔ DDEInitiate

The **DDEInitiate** function sets up a conversation between two applications. If this function is able to set up a channel, it returns the channel number. Otherwise it returns an error.

Syntax

```
DDEInitiate(<application>, <topic>)
```

`application`	is the name of the source application.
`topic`	refers to the data the channel must use (this is typically a file name).

Example

```
' Creating a DDE channel with the Excel worksheet
Channel = DDEInitiate("Excel", "Sheet1")
```

2. Conversation

➔ DDE

The **DDE** function starts a **DDE** conversation with another application, requests data from this application and displays it in a control on a form or report.

Syntax

```
DDE(<application>, <topic>, <item>)
```

`application`	is the name of the source application.
`topic`	is typically the name of a document or data file.
`item`	refers to a data item in the source application.

Example

```
' Assign the contents of the R1C1 cell
' to a text box via its ControlSource property.
= DDE("Excel", "Workbook1", "R1C1")
```

➔ DDESend

The **DDESend** function starts a **DDE** conversation with another application and sends data to this application from a control on a form or report.

Syntax

```
DDESend(<application>, <topic>, <item>, <data>)
```

`application`	is the name of the source application.
`topic`	is typically the name of a document or data file.
`item`	refers to a data item in the source application.
`data`	is a string or expression that contains the data you want to send to the application.

Example

```
' Assigning to the R1C1 cell,
' the contents of the City control
' via the ControlSource property of a text box.
= DDESend("Excel", "Workbook1", "R1C1", [City])
```

→ DDEPoke

The **DDEPoke** statement sends information to the source application across an open channel.

Syntax

```
DDEPoke <channel_number>, <item>, <data>
```

`channel_number`	is the number of the channel that the **DDEInitiate** function returned.
`item`	refers to a data item in the source application.
`data`	is the data you want to send to the source application.

Example

```
' Sending the value 15 to the cell R1C1
DDEPoke Channel, "R1C1", "15"
```

→ DDERequest

The **DDERequest** function requests information from a source application.

Syntax

```
DDERequest(<channel_number>, <item>)
```

`channel_number` is the number of the channel that the **DDEInitiate** function returned.

`item` refers to a data item in the source application.

Example

```
' Assigning the contents of the R1C1 cell
' to the Amount variable
Amount = DDERequest (Channel, "R1C1")
```

➔ DDEExecute

The **DDEExecute** statement sends a command to the source application across an open DDE channel.

Syntax

```
DDEExecute (<channel_number>, <command>)
```

`channel_number` is the number of the channel that the **DDEInitiate** function returned.

`command` is a string containing a command that the source application will recognize.

Example

```
' Creating a new worksheet
DDEExecute Channel, "[New(1)]"
```

3. Termination

➔ DDETerminate

The **DDETerminate** statement closes the DDE communications channel.

Syntax

```
DDETerminate (<channel_number>)
```

`channel_number` is the number of the channel that the **DDEInitiate** function returned.

Example

```
' Closing the DDE channel
DDETerminate Channel
```

➔ DDETerminateAll

The **DDETerminateAll** statement closes all the DDE communications channels.

Syntax

```
DDETerminateAll
```

4. Overall example

This example displays the contents of an Access table in Excel.

```
Private Sub TransferXLS_Clients()

' Access object variables
Dim dbs As DAO.Database
Dim rstClient As DAO.Recordset
Dim fld As DAO.Field

' DDE variables
Dim Channel As Variant
Dim intRow As Integer
Dim intCol As Integer
Dim strPosition As String

' Excel variables
Dim strExcel As String
Dim blnRes As Boolean

On Error Resume Next

' Opening the Clients table
Set dbs = CurrentDb
Set rstClient = dbs.OpenRecordset("Clients", dbOpenTable)

' Opening a DDE channel to Excel
Channel = DDEInitiate("Excel", "Sheet1")

' In the case of an error, start the Excel application
If Err Then
    Err = 0

                                                  .../...
```

```
.../...
'   Searching for the Excel application
    With Application.FileSearch
        .NewSearch
        .LookIn = "C:\"
        .SearchSubFolders = True
        .Filename = "Excel.exe"
        .FileType = "*.exe"
        If .Execute() > 0 Then
            strExcel = .FoundFiles(1)
        End If
    End With

' Starting Excel
    blnRes = Shell(strExcel, vbNormalFocus)
    If Not blnRes Then
        MsgBox "Excel application not found", vbExclamation
        Exit Sub
    End If
    Channel = DDEInitiate("Excel", "Sheet1")
End If

' Activating the Excel window
intRow = 1
intCol = 1

' Setting the column headers to field names
For Each fld In rstClient.Fields
    strPosition = "R" & intRow & "C" & intCol
    DDEPoke Channel, strPosition, rstClient.Fields(intCol - 1).Name
    intCol = intCol + 1
Next fld

                                                            .../...
```

```
.../...
' Scrolling through the records that must be sent
Do While Not rstClient.EOF
    intRow = intRow + 1
    intCol = 1
    For Each fld In rstClient.Fields
        strPosition = "R" & intRow & "C" & intCol
        DDEPoke Channel, strPosition, rstClient(intCol - 1)
        intCol = intCol + 1
    Next fld
    rstClient.MoveNext
Loop

End Sub
```

Chapter 11: Internet programming

A. Customizing data access pages

The **DataAccessPage** object represents a data access page in Microsoft Access. The **ActiveDataAccessPage** property of the **Screen** object indicates the active data access page.

1. Properties not available in Design View

Application	allows you to access the Microsoft Access **Application** object.
ConnectionString	returns the connection string to the Microsoft Access **DataAccessPage** object.
CurrentView	returns the current view of the **DataAccessPage** object.
Document	allows you to access the Microsoft Internet Explorer 5.0 Dynamic HTML **Document** object for HTML pages.
Parent	refers to the parent object.
WindowHeight	indicates the height of a **DataAccessPage** object in twips.
WindowWidth	indicates the width of a **DataAccessPage** object in twips.

2. Methods

ApplyTheme indicates the Microsoft Office theme for a specific **DataAccessPage** object.

B. WebOptions object

A **WebOptions** object refers to the option properties of a specific data access page (**DataAccessPage** object).

Properties

Application allows you to access the Microsoft Access **Application** object.

Download Components sets or indicates whether or not the Microsoft Office tools will be downloaded automatically with the Web page.

Encoding indicates the encoding for a **DataAccessPage** object.

FolderSuffix indicates the folder suffix that Microsoft Access uses when you save a **DataAccessPage** object as a Web page.

LocationOf Components sets or indicates the access path to the Microsoft Office controls that users can download.

OrganizeInFolder specifies where supporting files are stored.

Parent refers to the parent object.

UseLongFileNames specifies whether or not long file names are used when you store a document as a **DataAccessPage** object.

Methods

UseDefaultFolder Suffix indicates for the specified **DataAccessPage** object, the default suffix for the folder containing the files for the language support you have selected or installed.

C. Importing and exporting data in XML format

XML (*eXtensible Markup Language*) is the standard language for describing and exchanging data on the Web, while HTML (*HyperText Markup Language*) is the standard language for creating and displaying Web pages.

Complementary to XML, XSL (*eXtensible Stylesheet Language*) allows you to control and present XML documents.

Microsoft Access 2002 allows you to import and export data as XML files, and presentation styles as XSL files.

In VBA, the **Application** object provides the **ImportXML** and **ExportXML** methods to import and export data in XML format.

1. ExportXML method

The **ExportXML** method exports the data and/or presentation styles of a specific Access object. You can export the following Access objects in XML format:

- tables,
- queries,
- forms,
- reports,
- data access pages.

Syntax

```
Application.ExportXML(<ObjectType>, <DataSource>,
[<DataTarget>], [<SchemaTarget>],
[<PresentationTarget>], [<ImageTarget>], [<Encoding>],
[<OtherFlags>])
```

`ObjectType`	(required) indicates the type of Access object for export (**acExportDataAccessPage**, **acExportForm**, **acExportReport**, etc.)
`DataSource`	(required) is a string that contains the name of the Access object for export.
`DataTarget`	(optional) is a string that contains the name of the filename or path for the data you want to export: if you omit this argument the data will not be exported.

`SchemaTarget`	(optional) is a string that contains the name of the filename or path for the exported schema information: if you omit this argument, this information will be included in the data document.
`PresentationTarget`	(optional) is a string that contains the name of the filename or path for the exported presentation information: if you omit this argument the data will not be exported.
`ImageTarget`	(optional) indicates the path for the exported images: if you omit this argument the images will not be exported.
`Encoding`	(optional) indicates the text encoding for the exported XML file.
`OtherFlags`	(optional) is a long integer that represents the sum of the value options that you can choose from the following list:

Value	Description
1	**Related tables**: includes the different tables for the object that DataSource specifies.
2	**Relational properties**: creates relational schema properties.
4	**Run from server**: creates an ASP wrapper and defaults to an HTML wrapper; this option applies only when you are exporting reports.
8	**Special properties**: creates extended property schema properties.

2. ImportXML method

The **ImportXML** method imports the data and/or presentation styles from an XML file into a Microsoft Access table.

Syntax

```
Application.ImportXML(<DataSource>, [<ImportOptions>])
```

`DataSource`	(required) is a string that contains the name and path of the XML file for import.
`ImportOptions`	(optional) defines options for importing XML files.

Constants for defining ImportOptions:

`acAppendData`	if there is already a table with the same name as the XML file, the data is added to this table. Otherwise, the table is created.
`acStructureAndData`	(default value) This option imports the structure and the data. If there is already a table with the same name as the XML file, Access generates a new table.
`acStructureOnly`	this option imports only the structure. If there is already a table with the same name as the XML file, Access generates a new table.

3. XML import/export example

This example carries out the following steps:

- exporting a table in XML format,
- displaying the XML file in the Internet Explorer,
- exporting a form presentation,
- importing the XML file into a new table, after changing its contents.

To carry out this example, you must create the "C:\XML" folder and copy, the Northwind.mdb database (which Access 2002 provides) into this folder.

Step 1: Exporting the Customers table

Enter the following code in a new module called **ImportExportXML** and run the **ExportCustomersTable** procedure.

```
Private Sub ExportCustomersTable()
'   Exporting the Customers table
    ExportTable ("Customers")
End Sub

Private Sub ExportTable(strTableName As String)
' Exporting data (XML) and their presentation (XSL)
Application.ExportXML _
    ObjectType:=acExportTable, _
    DataSource:=strTableName, _
    DataTarget:="C:\XML\" & strTableName & ".xml", _
    PresentationTarget:="C:\XML\" & strTableName & ".xsl", _
    Encoding:=acUTF8
End Sub
```

Step 2: Linking the XML and XSL files

Step 1 created the following three files in the XML folder: **customers.xml**, **customers.xsl** and **customers.htm**.

If you open the **customers.xml** file in the Internet Explorer, you will obtain the following result:

To view the list of customers properly, you must use the **customers.htm** file which links the **xml** file and the **xsl** file. Alternatively, you can modify the **customers.xml** file, in order to associate the **customers.xsl** file with it (by adding a new line after the first line as shown below).

To change the code in the **xml** or **xsl** file, you can use a text editor, such as Windows **Notepad**.

```
<?xml version="1.0" encoding="UTF-8"?>
<?xml-stylesheet type="text/xsl" href="Customers.xsl"?>
<dataroot xmlns:od="urn:schemas-microsoft-com:officedata">
<Customers>
```

Step 3: Exporting a form presentation

Enter the following code in the **ImportExportXML** module and run the **ExportCustomersForm** procedure.

```
Private Sub ExportCustomersForm()
'   Exporting the Customers table
    ExportForm("Customers")
End Sub

Private Sub ExportForm(strFormName As String)
'   Exporting the (XSL) form presentation
    Application.ExportXML _
    ObjectType:=acExportForm, _
    DataSource:=strFormName, _
    PresentationTarget:="C:\XML\" & strFormName & ".xsl", _
    Encoding:=acUTF8
End Sub
```

The **ExportCustomersForm** procedure has replaced the **customers.xsl** file in the **C:\XML** folder. If you open the **customers.xml** file in the Internet Explorer now, you will obtain the following result:

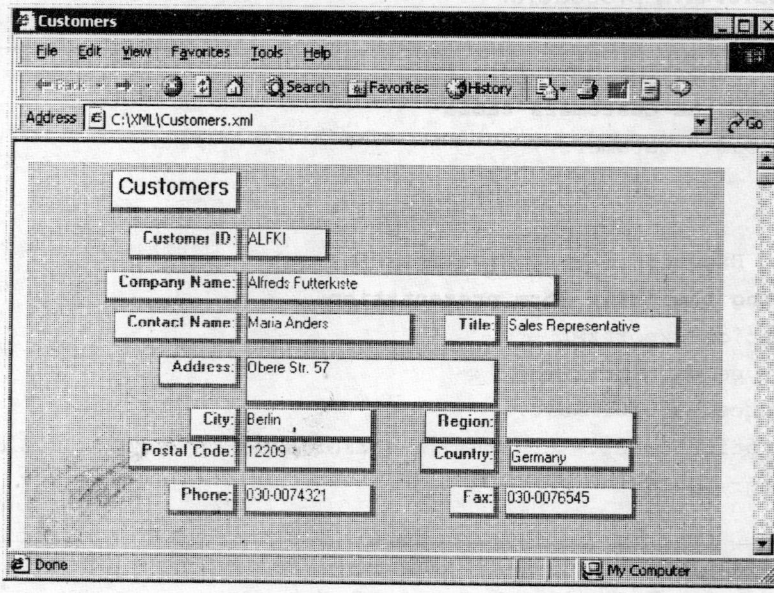

Step 4: Importing the customers.xml file after modification

Edit the **customers.xml** file so that it contains only the first record.

```
<?xml version="1.0" encoding="UTF-8"?>
<?xml-stylesheet type="text/xsl" href="Customers.xsl"?>
<dataroot xmlns:od="urn:schemas-microsoft-com:officedata">
<Customers>
<CustomerID>ALFKI</CustomerID>
<CompanyName>Alfreds Futterkiste</CompanyName>
<ContactName>Maria Anders</ContactName>
<ContactTitle>Sales Representative</ContactTitle>
<Address>Obere Str. 57</Address>
                                                       .../...
```

```
.../...
<City>Berlin</City>
<PostalCode>12209</PostalCode>
<Country>Germany</Country>
<Phone>030-0074321</Phone>
<Fax>030-0076545</Fax>
</Customers>
</dataroot>
```

Enter the following code in the **ImportExportXML** module and run the **ImportCustomersTable** procedure (after saving your **Customers** table under another name in Access).

```
Private Sub ImportCustomersTable()
'    Importing the Customers table
     ImportTable ("Customers")
End Sub

Private Sub ImportTable(strTableName As String)
'    Importing the (XSL) form presentation
     Application.ImportXML "C:\XML\" & strTableName & ".xml"
End Sub
```

The **ImportCustomersTable** procedure has created the **Customers** table in Access with only one record.

D.Creating an HTML file (example)

You can use VBA to create an HTML file. For this purpose, you must use the **FileSystemObject** object.

Chapter 12 describes the methods and properties of this object.

The following example creates the **ImageList.htm** file and copies into it all the images in the folder selected by the user.

```
Private Sub CreateHTML()
Dim fso As Object
' Folder
Dim fld As Object
' Files Collection
Dim fls As Object
' File Object
Dim fl As Object
' Html file
Dim fHtml As Object
Dim strFolder As String
Dim strHtml As String

' Selecting the folder
strFolder = InputBox("Enter the path to the folder " _
& "that contains the images", "VBA Test", "C:\")
' Finding the image files
Set fso = CreateObject("Scripting.FileSystemObject")
If fso.folderExists(strFolder) Then
   Set fld = fso.GetFolder(strFolder & "\")
   Set fls = fld.Files
   strHtml = "<html>"
```

.../...

```
.../...

    For Each fl In fls
        If Left(fl.Type, 5) = "Image" Then
            strHtml = strHtml & "<img src=" & "'" _
            & strFolder & "\" _
            & fl.Name & "' height=" & x & 100 & x & ">" _
            & fl.Name & "<BR>"
        End If
    Next
    ' Creating the HTML file
    strHtml = strHtml & "</html>"
    Set fHtml = fso.CreateTextFile(strFolder & "\" & _
    "ImageList.htm", True)
    fHtml.Write (strHtml)
Else
    MsgBox strFolder & " folder not found"
End If

End Sub
```

Here is an Internet Explorer preview of an HTML file that this example created:

Chapter 12: Windows programming

A. Introducing APIs

Windows API (*Application Programming Interface*) allows you to control the most internal aspects of the operating system. You can extend and customize your Access applications by calling Windows API functions from your VBA code. Although Microsoft Access continues to develop and its native programming language (VBA) offers more and more system functions, you still need to run API functions to carry out certain tasks.

An API is a set of functions that you can use to work with a component, an application or the operating system. An API is generally made up of one or more DLLs (*Dynamic Link Libraries*).

Windows API is the most commonly used API. It contains the DLLs of the Windows operating system. Each Windows application interacts directly or indirectly with the Windows API. This approach ensures the coherency of all the applications that run on Windows.

Here are the most commonly used Windows DLLs:

Kernel32.dll handles low level operating system operations such as memory and resource management.

User32.dll handles Windows management operations concerning messages, clocks, menus, communication and so forth.

GDI32.dll is a GDI (*Graphics Device Interface*) library that handles operations to output devices (managing graphical objects, display contexts and fonts).

Windows provides other APIs such as the **MAPI** (*Mail Application Programming Interface*), for example, which you can use to create **e-mail applications**.

For information on Windows API features, you can consult two sources:

- **API Viewer** (composed of the ApiLoad.exe executable file that Microsoft Office XP Developer and Microsoft Visual Basic provide) displays constants, declarations and API types. You can select items in the API Viewer and copy them to VBA applications.
  You can find information on the API Viewer in text files such as win32api.txt and mapi32.txt. For ease of viewing, you can import these files into an mdb database.
- **Microsoft SDK** (*Software Development Kit*) provides full documentation on Windows API. The **Microsoft Developer Network** Web site offers this kit free of charge.

B. Calling Windows API functions

To call a Windows API function, you must declare it using the **Declare** statement in the declarations section of one your project's modules (generally, in a module that contains your application's general procedures).

1. Syntax of the Declare statement

In the 32-bit version of Visual Basic, DLL function and procedure names are case-sensitive.

```
[Public | Private] Declare Sub <procedure_name> Lib
"<DLL_name>" [Alias "<alias_name>"] [([argument_list])]
```

or,

```
[Public | Private] Declare Function <function_name> Lib
"<DLL_name>"

[Alias "<alias_name>"] [([argument_list])] [As <type>]
```

`procedure_name`, `function_name`	is the name of the procedure or function, as it appears in the VBA code.
`DLL_name`	is the name of the DLL.
`alias_name`	is the name of the procedure or the function, as it appears in the DLL.
`argument_list`	is the list of arguments you must pass to the procedure when you call it (cf. Chapter 2 - Visual Basic language).
`Type`	is the type of the Function procedure's return value.

Some DLLs use ordinal numbers instead of names for their procedures. You can use the same syntax to declare such procedures, but you must define the **alias_name** as this ordinal number, prefixed by a hash (#) character (for example: "#52").

2. Passing arguments

Most DLL functions and procedures use C language syntax, as they are written in this language. Because of this, passing arguments to a DLL function or procedure is not always a simple matter. With DLLs that use C syntax, you must pass all arguments by value except for array arguments.

The C language considers a string to be an array of characters.

Some DLL procedure arguments can accept different data types (as with the Variant type in VBA). You must declare such variables using the **Any** type (for example: `variable As Any`). By default, Visual Basic passes arguments by reference. To pass an argument by value you must state your purpose explicitly using the `ByVal` clause, when you call the procedure or function.

Argument declaration table

C language declaration	Visual Basic declaration	What you pass
Bool	ByVal <variable> As Boolean	an expression producing a Boolean type value.
LONG, DWORD, COLORREF	ByVal <variable> As Long	an expression producing a Long type value.
WORD	ByVal <variable> As Long	an expression producing a Long type value.
NULL	As Any or ByVal <variable> As Long	ByVal Nothing or ByVal O$ or vbNullString.
int, short	ByVal <variable> As Integer	an expression producing an Integer type value.
char, BYTE	ByVal <variable> As Byte	an expression producing a Byte type value.

C language declaration	Visual Basic declaration	What you pass
Long integer (int, uint) a 32-bit integer with a 32-bit compiler	ByVal <variable> As Long	an expression producing a Long type value.
Windows identifier (hWnd, hDC, hMenu, etc).	ByVal <variable> As Long	an expression producing a Long type value.
Empty (return value for a function)	Sub <procedure>	not applicable.
Pointer to a string (LPSTR)	ByVal <variable> As String	an expression producing a String type value.
Pointer to a long integer (LPDWORD)	<variable> As Long	a Long type value.
Empty pointer	<variable> As Any	a variable (use ByVal to pass a string).
Character pointer	<variable> As Byte	an expression producing a Byte type value.
Long Integer pointer (LPINT)	<variable> As Long	an expression producing a Long type value.
Structure pointer	<variable> As <Type>	a variable of this user-defined type.

C. API Windows functions

Here is a list of commonly used Windows API functions. The next section contains examples that use some of these functions.

GetWindowsDirectory() returns the fully qualified path to the Windows directory (which contains applications and system tools).

GetSystemDirectory() returns the fully qualified path to the Windows system directory (which contains DLLs, etc.).

GetSystemInfo() returns information on the system, in a SYSTEM_INFO type structure.

GetActiveWindow() returns a handle to the active window.

FindWindow() returns a handle to a window, according to the window's name and/or class you specify.

SetFocus gives the input focus to the window identified by its handle.

GetPrivateProfileString returns a string value from an INI file, according to a section name and a key.

WNetGetUser returns the network user name.

D.Examples of using API Windows functions

1. Getting the Windows directory

Declaring the API function

```
' This API function returns the Windows directory
Private Declare Function GetWindowsDirectory Lib "kernel32" _
    Alias "GetWindowsDirectoryA" _
    (ByVal lpWindowsDir As String, _
    ByVal lpWindowsHeight As Long)
    As Long
```

Calling the API function

```
Function GetWinPath() As String

' The VBA function returns the Windows directory
Dim strResult As String
Dim strProfile As String

strResult = String(255, " ")
strProfile = GetWindowsDirectory(strResult, 255)

' Truncate the string on the first null character
If strProfile = "" Then
    GetWinPath = ""
Else
                                                        .../...
```

```
.../...
    strResult = Trim(strResult)
    GetWinPath = Left(strResult, InStr(1, _
    strResult, vbNullChar) - 1)
End If
End Function
```

2. Starting the Excel application

This example checks to see if the Excel application is active and starts it if it is not.

This example uses two API functions: **FindWindow**, which looks for the Excel window and **FindExecutable**, which looks for the Excel.exe file.

Declaring the API function

```
' This API function looks for a window
Public Declare Function FindWindow Lib "user32" _
    Alias "FindWindowA" (ByVal lpClassName As String, _
    ByVal lpWindowName As String) As Long

' This API function looks for an executable file
Public Declare Function FindExecutable Lib "shell32.dll" _
    Alias "FindExecutableA" (ByVal lpFile As String, _
    ByVal lpDirectory As String, _
    ByVal lpResult As String) As Long
```

Calling the API function

```
Private Function StartExcel() As Boolean
Dim strClassName As String
Dim strWindowName As String
Dim Hwnd As Long
Dim blnExe As Boolean
Dim strExcelDir As String
Dim Result As Long
' Initializing
StartExcel = False

' Looking for an active Excel window
strClassName = vbNullString
strWindowName = "Microsoft Excel - Workbook1"
Hwnd = FindWindow(strClassName, strWindowName)

' If an active Excel window is not found,
'    look for the Excel directory and start Excel
If Hwnd = 0 Then
    strExcelDir = String$(255, 0)
    Result = FindExecutable("Excel.exe", "C:\", strExcelDir)
    If Result = 0 Then Exit Function
    blnExe = Shell(strExcelDir, vbNormalFocus)
    If Not blnExe Then Exit Function
End If
StartExcel = True


End Function
```

3. Getting a value from an INI file

The AppInvoices.ini file contains the following three lines:

```
[BASE]
BasePath="C:\Invoices"
BaseName="Invoices.mdb"
```

The following example gets the name and access path from the AppInvoices.ini file, which resides in the Windows directory (by calling the GetWinPath function, as in the first example).

Declaring the API function

```
Public Declare Function GetPrivateProfileString Lib "kernel32" _
    Alias "GetPrivateProfileStringA" _
    (ByVal lpApplicationName As String, _
    ByVal lpKeyName As Any, _
    ByVal lpDefault As String, _
    ByVal lpReturnedString As String, _
    ByVal nSize As Long, _
    ByVal lpFileName As String) As Long
```

Calling the API function

```
Public Function ReadKey(Section As String, Key As String, _
File As String) As String

' This function returns the value of the key in an .ini file
Dim strResult As String
Dim strProfile As Integer
```

.../...

```
.../...
Dim i As Integer
strResult = String(255, " ")
strProfile = GetPrivateProfileString(Section, Key, "", _
          strResult, 255, File)
If strProfile = 0 Then
    ReadKey = ""
    Exit Function
End If

' Truncating the string on the first null character
strResult = Trim(strResult)
ReadKey = Left(strResult, _
InStr(1, strResult, vbNullChar) - 1)

End Function
```

Calling the ReadKey VBA function.

```
Private Sub Init_Projet()
Dim strDBName As String
Dim strPath As String
Dim strWinPath As String

' Looking for the database name and directory
strWinPath = GetWinPath()
If strWinPath = "" Then Exit Sub

' Looking for values in Invoices.ini
strDBName = Trim(ReadKey("DB", "DBName", strWinPath _
                        & "\" & "Invoices.ini"))
strPath = Trim(ReadKey("DB", "DBPATH", strWinPath _
                        & "\" & "Invoices.ini"))

End Sub
```

E. FileSystemObject object

The **FileSystemObject** object accesses the computer's file system. You can use it to look for, create, delete and move files and folders.

1. Methods

File methods

CopyFile copies one or more files from one folder to another.

CreateTextFile creates a file with a specific name and returns a **TextStream** object that you can use to read from or write to the file.

DeleteFile deletes a specific file.

FileExists returns a Boolean value that indicates whether or not the file exists.

MoveFile moves one or more files from one folder to another.

OpenTextFile opens a specific file and returns a **TextStream** object that you can use to read from or write to the file.

Folder methods

CopyFolder moves a folder from one location to another.

CreateFolder creates a folder.

DeleteFolder deletes a specific folder and its contents.

FolderExists returns a Boolean value that indicates whether or not the folder exists.

MoveFolder moves one or more folders from one location to another.

Drive methods

DriveExists returns a Boolean value that indicates whether or not the drive exists.

GetDrive returns a **Drive** object corresponding to the drive on the specified path.

GetDriveName returns a string containing the name of the drive on the specified path.

Properties

Drives returns the collection of all the **Drive** objects that the local machine offers.

2. Example

The following example lists all the available drives and the amount of free space on each.

```
Sub ShowDrive()
Dim fso As Object
Dim strMsg As String
Dim drv As Object
Dim drvs As Object

Set fs = CreateObject("Scripting.FileSystemObject")
Set drvs = fs.Drives
For Each drv In drvs
    If drv.isready Then
        strMsg = strMsg & drv.driveletter & ": " _
        & Format(FreeSpace(drv.driveletter & ":"), _
        "# ### ##0") & " KBytes" & vbCrLf
    End If
Next
MsgBox strMsg
End Sub

Private Function FreeSpace(drvPath)
Dim fso As Object
Dim drv As Object
Set fso = CreateObject("Scripting.FileSystemObject")
Set drv = fso.GetDrive(fso.GetDriveName(drvPath))
FreeSpace = drv.FreeSpace / 1024
End Function
```

Chapter 13: Example of a mini-application

A. Overview

1. Scenario

The Human Resources department in a company wants to manage the training courses that the company employees will follow.

This chapter describes an Access application that was set up for this purpose. This application allows you to:

- enter details on training courses,
- search for training courses according to different criteria,
- print the corresponding list of training courses along with the criteria that were used to select them.

2. Training database

This application uses the Training database. This database offers two forms and one report:

- The Courses form allows you to enter, modify and delete training courses.
- The Search form allows you to find training courses according to different criteria.
- The Courses report displays the list of training courses selected in the Search form.

The **Cascade Delete Related Records** option is active on the relationship between the Courses table and the Participants table.

3. Relational model of the database

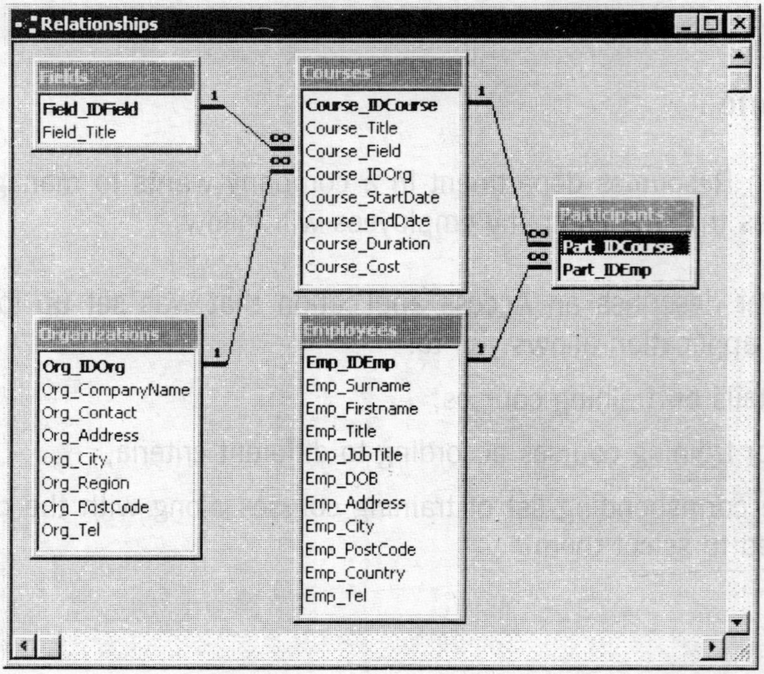

B. Courses form

To add courses to your database, you can open this form directly from Access. To modify or delete an existing course, you can call this form from the Search form.

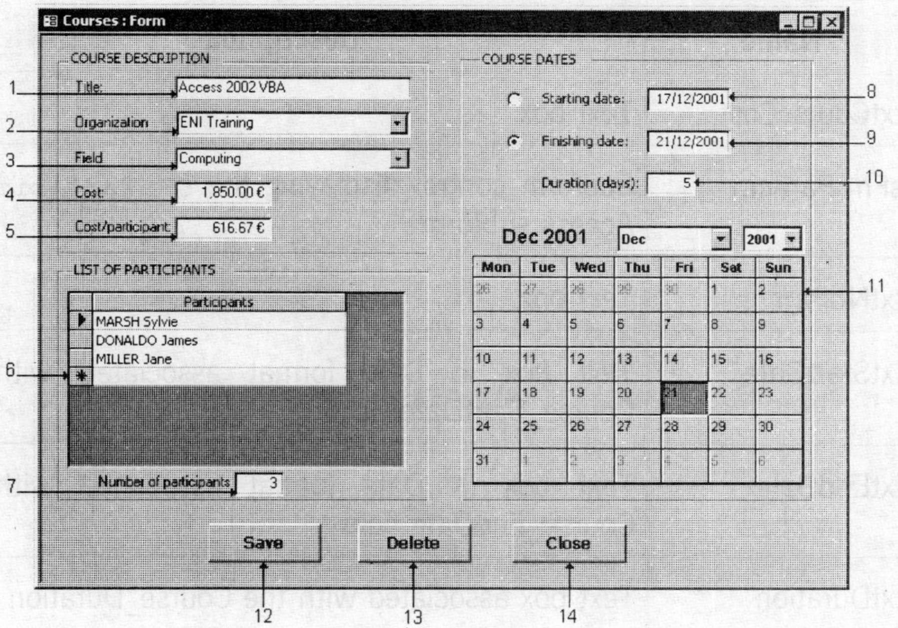

The record source of this form is the Courses table.

1. List of controls

	Name	Description
1	txtTitle	Text box associated with the Course_Title field
2	cboOrganization	Drop-down list box based on the Organizations table and associated with the Course_IDOrg field
3	cboField	Drop-down list box based on the Fields table and associated with the Course_Field field
4	txtCost	Text box associated with the Course_Cost field

	Name	Description
5	txtCourseCost	Text box
6	sFrmParticip	Subform control displaying the `SF Participants` Access subform
7	txtNbPart	Text box
8	txtStartDate	Text box in Date format associated with the Course_StartDate field
9	txtEndDate	Text box in Date format associated with the Course_EndDate field
10	txtDuration	Text box associated with the Course_Duration field
11	Calendar	Calendar control (msCal.ocx ActiveX supplied with Access)
12	cmdSave	Command button
13	cmdDelete	Command button
14	cmdClose	Command button

Control	Specific properties
Form	Data entry = Yes Source = Courses
txtNbPart	Default value = 0 Locked = Yes Control Source = [sFrmParticipant].[Form]![txtNbPart]
txtCourseCost	Locked = Yes

2. VBA code

The VBA code associated with this form includes the following features:

- synchronization between form and subform: when you add or delete a participant, the number of participants and the cost per participant are recalculated and redisplayed,
- handling of duplication at subform level,
- use of calendar controls for entering dates,
- use of a function for date calculations.

General VBA code: common procedures and declarations

Include the following code in a standard module (for example, GenProc).

```
Option Compare Database
Option Explicit
Public p_strCond As String

Function NbWorkDays(Date1, Date2) As Integer

Dim NbDays, NbWeeks As Integer
'   Calculating the number of week days
'   excluding Saturdays and Sundays
NbDays = DateDiff("d", Date1, Date2) + 1
'   Number of Sundays between the 2 dates
NbWeeks = DateDiff("ww", Date1, Date2)
NbWorkDays = NbDays - (NbWeeks * 2)

End Function
```

VBA code for the form

```
Option Explicit
Dim mblnUpd As Boolean

Private Sub Calendar_Click()
Dim intDuration As Integer
'   Modifying the date according to the chkDates option
If chkDates = 1 Then
   txtStartDate.Value = Calendar.Value
   chkDates = 2
```

.../...

```
.../...
Else
   txtEndDate.Value = Calendar.Value
End If

'   If both dates have been entered
'   check the dates and the duration
If txtStartDate <> "" And txtEndDate <> "" Then
   intDuration = DateValue(txtEndDate) - DateValue(txtStartDate)
   If intDuration <= 0 Then
      MsgBox "The Starting date must be earlier than " _
      & "the Finishing date", vbCritical, "Course Management"
      Exit Sub
   Else
      txtDuration = NbWorkDays(DateValue(txtStartDate), _
                    DateValue(txtEndDate))
   End If
End If
End Sub

Private Sub cmdSave_Click()
Dim intRep As String
'   Checking required fields
If Not Ctrl_Info Then Exit Sub
If IsNull(txtStartDate) Or IsNull(txtEndDate <> "") Then
   If MsgBox("Dates not entered, validate " _
      & "the update?", vbQuestion & vbYesNo) = vbNo Then
      txtEndDate.SetFocus
      Exit Sub
   End If
End If
'   Saving the course
DoCmd.Save
                                                  .../...
```

```
.../...

'   Start creating a new course, if DataEntry mode
If Me.DataEntry Then
   txtDuration = ""
   txtCourseCost = ""
   mblnUpd = False
   DoCmd.GoToRecord , , acNewRec
   txtTitle.SetFocus
   cmdDelete.Enabled = False
   cmdSave.Enabled = False
Else
   DoCmd.Close
End If
End Sub

Private Sub cmdClose_Click()
'   If course is being entered
If txtTitle <> "" Then
   MsgBox ("Save or delete the course before closing")
Else
   DoCmd.Close
End If
End Sub

Private Sub CmdDelete_Click()
On Error GoTo Err_Del
If mblnUpd Then
   '   Deleting the record if saved
   Me.txtTitle.SetFocus
   DoCmd.DoMenuItem acFormBar, acEditMenu, 8, , acMenuVer70
   DoCmd.DoMenuItem acFormBar, acEditMenu, 6, , acMenuVer70
                                                    .../...
```

```
.../...
Else
   '   Otherwise, cancel the entry
   DoCmd.DoMenuItem acFormBar, acEditMenu, acUndo, , acMenuVer70
End If
On Error GoTo 0
Exit Sub

Err_Del:
   MsgBox "Cannot delete: " & Err.Number, vbCritical
   On Error GoTo 0
   End Sub

Private Sub Form_AfterUpdate()
'   Updating flag
mblnUpd = True
End Sub

Private Sub Form_Load()
'   Initializing the Calendar
Calendar.Value = Date
'   Deactivating the Cancel and Save buttons
'   if DataEntry mode
cmdDelete.Enabled = False
If Me.DataEntry Then
   cmdSave.Enabled = False
   cmdDelete.Enabled = False
Else
   '  Calculating the cost/participant
   Me.Recalc
   If txtNbPart > 0 Then
      txtCourseCost = txtCost / txtNbPart
   End If
End If
End Sub                                                    .../...
```

```
.../...

Private Sub sFrmParticipant_Enter()
'   Checking the entry
Ctrl_Info
End Sub

Private Sub txtCost_AfterUpdate()
'   Calculating the cost/participant
If txtCost > 0 And txtNbPart > 0 Then
   txtCourseCost = txtCost / txtNbPart
End If
End Sub

Private Sub txtTitle_BeforeUpdate(Cancel As Integer)
'   Activating the Cancel button
cmdDelete.Enabled = True
End Sub

Private Function Ctrl_Info() As Boolean
'   Checking if required fields have been entered
Ctrl_Info = False
If IsNull(txtTitle) Then
   MsgBox "You must enter the title", vbCritical
   txtTitle.SetFocus
   Exit Function
End If
If IsNull(cboOrganization) Then
   MsgBox "You must enter the organization", vbCritical
   cboOrganization.SetFocus
   Exit Function
End If
                                                    .../...
```

```
.../...
If IsNull(cboField) Then
   MsgBox "You must enter the field", vbCritical
   cboField.SetFocus
   Exit Function
End If
If IsNull(txtCost) Then
   MsgBox "You must enter the course cost", vbCritical
   txtCost.SetFocus
   Exit Function
End If
Ctrl_Info = True
End Function
```

3. SF Participants subform

The **Courses** form and the **SF Participants** subform are linked via the Course_IDCourse and Part_IDCourse fields.

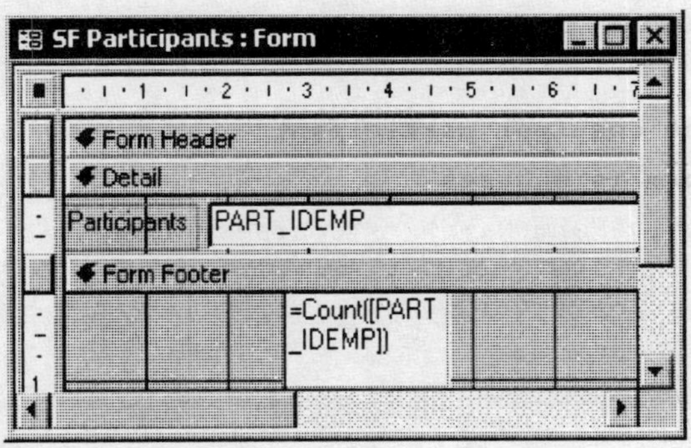

	Name	Description
1	cboEmployee	Drop-down list box based on the Employees table and associated with the PART_IDEmp field
2	txtNbPart	Unbound list box

Control	Specific properties
Form	Source = Participants
txtNbPart	Control Source = Count([PART_IDEmp])

4. VBA code

```
Private Sub cboEmployee_AfterUpdate()
'    If Duplicates: Refresh method failure
On Error GoTo Duplicates
Me.Refresh
On Error GoTo 0
'    Recalculate the cost per participant
'    If the main form is Courses
If UCase(Screen.ActiveForm.Name) = "Courses" Then
   CalcCourseCost
End If
Exit Sub

'    Handling Duplicates: error message
Duplicates:
If Err.Number = 3022 Then
   MsgBox "Participant already entered"                    .../...
```

```
.../...
Else
   MsgBox "Error adding the participant: " _
   & Err.Number, vbCritical
End If
'   Clearing the field
cboEmployee = ""
End Sub

Private Sub Form_AfterDelConfirm(Status As Integer)
'   Recalculate the cost per participant
'   If the main form is Courses
If UCase(Screen.ActiveForm.Name) = "Courses" Then
   CalcCourseCost
End If
End Sub

Private Sub CalcCourseCost()
Dim frmFormat As Object
'   Calculating the cost/participant
Set frmFormat = Forms![Courses]
frmFormat.Recalc
If frmFormat.txtCost <> 0 And txtNbPart <> 0 Then
   frmFormat.txtCostPart = frmFormat.txtCost / txtNbPart
End If
'   Activating the Save command button
If txtNbPart < > 0 Then frmFormat.cmdSave.Enabled = True
End Sub
```

C. Search form

This form displays and prints the list of courses that correspond to certain criteria. The Search form is not associated with a data source.

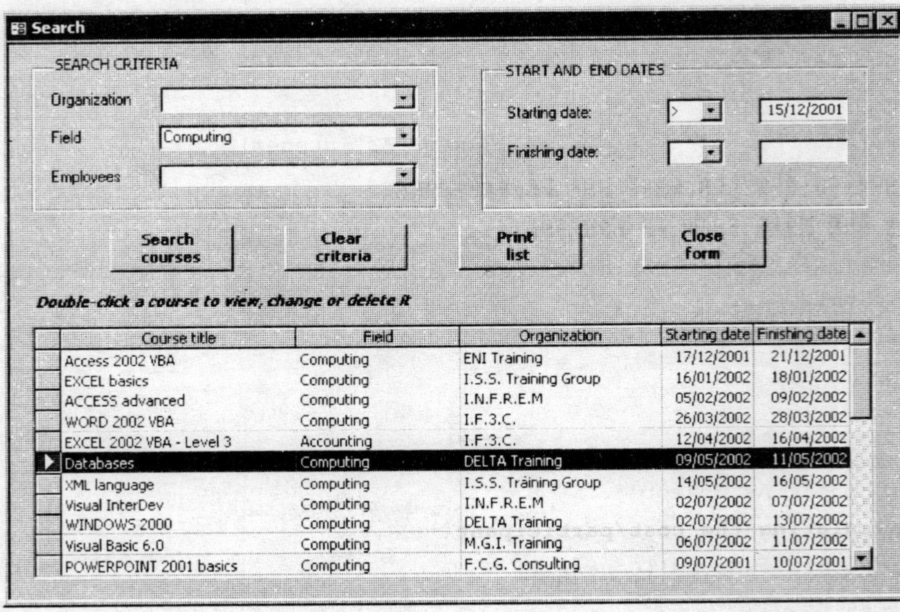

1. List of controls

	Name	Description
1	cboOrganization	Drop-down list based on the Organizations table
2	cboField	Drop-down list based on the Fields table
3	cboEmployee	Drop-down list based on the Employees table

	Name	Description
4	TxtStartDate	Text box in Date format
5	TxtOperat1	Drop-down list containing the values "=",">","<"
6	TxtEndDate	Text box in Date format associated with the Course_EndDate field
7	TxtOperat2	Drop-down list containing the values "=",">","<"
8	cmdSearch	Command button
9	cmdClear	Command button
10	cmdPrint	Command button
11	cmdClose	Command button
12	sFrmCourses	Subform control displaying the `SF Courses` Access subform

2. VBA code

The VBA code associated with this form has the following features:

- creation of an SQL query using the entered criteria,
- assigning the query to the subform to display only the required records,
- assigning the query to a report to print only the required records.

```
Option Compare Database
Option Explicit
Dim strSQL As String

Private Sub cmdSearch_Click()
'   Creating the query according to the entered criteria
If cboEmployee <> "" Then
   '   Courses, Participants and Employees tables
   strSQL = "SELECT COURSE_IDFORM, COURSE_TITLE, " _
   & "COURSE_FIELD, COURSE_IDORG, " _
   & "COURSE_STARTDATE, COURSE_ENDDATE FROM COURSES " _
   & "INNER JOIN (EMPLOYEES INNER JOIN PARTICIPANTS ON  " _
   & "EMPLOYEES.EMP_IDEMP = PARTICIPANTS.PART_IDEMP) " _
   & "ON (COURSES.COURSE_IDFORM = " _
   & "PARTICIPANTS.PART_IDFORM) "
Else
'  Courses table
   strSQL = "SELECT COURSE_IDFORM, COURSE_TITLE, " _
   & "COURSE_FIELD, COURSE_IDORG, " _
   & "COURSE_STARTDATE, COURSE_ENDDATE FROM COURSES "
End If
'   Concatenating the criteria
p_strCond = ""
If cboField <> "" Then
   p_strCond = p_strCond _
             & " AND COURSE_FIELD = " & cboField


End If
If cboOrganization <> "" Then
   p_strCond = p_strCond _
             & " AND COURSE_IDORG = " & cboOrganization
End If
If cboEmployee <> "" Then
   p_strCond = p_strCond _
             & " AND PART_IDEMP = " & cboEmployee
End If                                                       .../...
```

```
.../...
'   Date criteria
If cboOperat1 <> "" And txtStartDate <> "" Then
   p_strCond = p_strCond & " AND (COURSE_STARTDATE " _
   & cboOperat1 & " #" & Format(DateValue(txtStartDate), _
   "MM/DD/YY") & "#)"
End If
If cboOperat2 <> "" And txtEndDate <> "" Then
   p_strCond = p_strCond & " AND (COURSE_ENDDATE " & cboOperat2 _
   & " #" & Format(DateValue(txtEndDate), "MM/DD/YY") & "#)"
End If

'   Remplacing the 1st AND by WHERE
If p_strCond <> "" Then
   strSQL = strSQL & " WHERE " _
   & Right(p_strCond, (Len(p_strCond) - 4))
End If
'  Grouping by course
If cboEmployee <> "" Then
   strSQL = strSQL & " GROUP BY COURSE_IDFORM,COURSE_TITLE, " _
   & "COURSE_FIELD,COURSE_IDORG,COURSE_STARTDATE,COURSE_ENDDATE "
End If

'  Sorting by course start date
strSQL = strSQL & " ORDER BY COURSE_STARTDATE"

'   Assigning the conditions to the subform
[SFrmCOURSES].Form.RecordSource = strSQL
[SFrmCOURSES].Form.Requery
End Sub

Private Sub cmdClear_Click()
Dim ctl As Control                                              .../...
```

```
.../...
'   Clearing the text and list boxes
For Each ctl In Me.Controls
    If TypeOf ctl Is TextBox Or TypeOf ctl Is ComboBox Then
        ctl.Value = ""
    End If
Next
End Sub

Private Sub cmdPrint_Click()
'   Concatenating the criteria
p_strCond = ""
If cboField <> "" Then
    p_strCond = p_strCond & " - FIELD: " & cboField.Column(1)
End If
If cboOrganization <> "" Then
p_strCond = p_strCond & " - Organization: " & cboOrganization.Column(1)
End If
If cboEmployee <> "" Then
    p_strCond = p_strCond & " - Employee: " & cboEmployee.Column(1)
End If

'  Date criteria
If cboOperat1 <> "" And txtStartDate <> "" Then
    p_strCond = p_strCond & " - Start Date " & cboOperat1 _
            & " " & txtStartDate

End If
If cboOperat2 <> "" And txtEndDate <> "" Then
    p_strCond = p_strCond & " - End Date " & cboOperat1 _
            & " " & txtStartDate
End If
p_strCond = Right(p_strCond, Len(p_strCond) - 3)
                                                          .../...
```

```
.../...
'   Opening the report with the search criteria
DoCmd.OpenReport "Courses", acViewPreview, strSQL
End Sub

Private Sub cmdClose_Click()
DoCmd.Close
End Sub
```

3. SF Courses subform

The **SF Courses** subform is based on the Courses table.

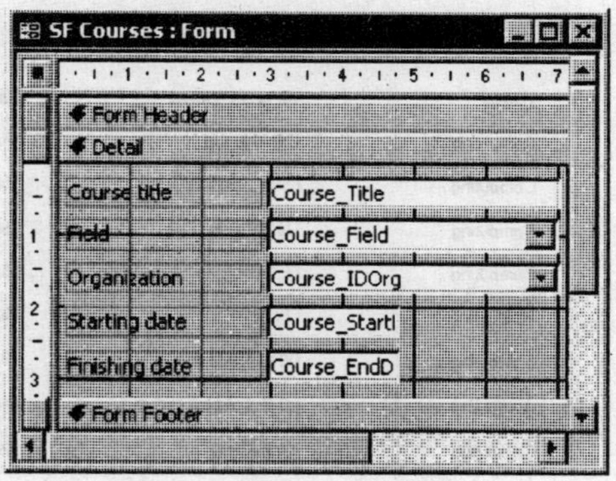

VBA code

```
Option Compare Database

Private Sub Form_DblClick(Cancel As Integer)
Dim lngIdForm As Long
                                        .../...
```

```
.../...
'   Displaying the Courses form
lngIdForm = [FOR_IDFORM]
DoCmd.OpenForm "Courses", acNormal, , _
"[COURSES_IDCOURSE]=" & lngIdForm, acFormEdit
End Sub
```

4. Courses report

The **Courses** report is based on the Courses table.

List of courses

Course title	*Field*	*Organization*	*Start date*	*End date*
Access 2002 VBA	Computing	ENI Training	17/12/2001	21/12/2001
EXCEL basics	Computing	I.S.S. Training Group	16/01/2002	18/01/2002
ACCESS advanced	Computing	I.N.F.R.E.M	05/02/2002	09/02/2002
WORD 2002 VBA	Computing	I.F.3.C.	26/03/2002	28/03/2002
EXCEL 2002 VBA - Level 3	Accounting	I.F.3.C.	12/04/2002	16/04/2002
Databases	Computing	DELTA Training	09/05/2002	11/05/2002
XML language	Computing	I.S.S. Training Group	14/05/2002	16/05/2002
Visual Interdev	Computing	I.N.F.R.E.M	02/07/2002	07/07/2002
WINDOWS 2000	Computing	DELTA Training	02/07/2002	13/07/2002
VISUAL BASIC 6.0	Computing	M.G.I. Training	06/07/2002	11/07/2002
POWERPOINT 2002 basics	Computing	F.C.G. Gonsulting	09/07/2002	10/07/2002

VBA code

```
Option Compare Database
Private Sub Report_Open(Cancel As Integer)
'   Assigning criteria upon opening
txtCriteria.Caption = p_strCond
End Sub
```

Appendices

A. VBA functions and statements

1. Handling strings

Functions

Format()	formats a string.
InStr()	finds a substring.
LCase()	converts to lower case.
Left()	extracts the left side of a string.
Len()	returns the length of a string.
LTrim()	removes leading spaces.
Mid()	returns a Variant (String) type value containing a specified number of characters from a string.
Right()	extracts the right side of a string.
RTrim()	removes trailing spaces.
Space()	creates a string of spaces.
StrComp()	compares two strings.
StrConv()	returns a Variant (String) type value converted to the indicated format.
String()	creates a repeating string.
Trim()	removes leading and trailing spaces.
UCase()	converts to upper case.

Statements

LSet left-aligns a string.

Option Compare declares the default comparison method.

RSet right-aligns a string.

2. Program sequencing and control

Functions

Choose() returns a value from a choose list according to an index.

DoEvents() stops running temporarily to allow the operating system to process other events.

IIF() returns a value according to a condition.

Switch() returns the value associated with the first true expression.

Statements

Call calls a Sub procedure.

Do ... Loop repeats a block of statements while, or until, a condition is **True**.

End ends a procedure or a block.

Exit Do leaves a **Do ... Loop** block

Exit For leaves a **For ... Next** block.

For Each ... Next	repeats a block of statements for each item in an array or a collection.
For ... Next	repeats a block of statements a set number of times.
Function ... End Function	defines the beginning and end of a function.
GoSub ... Return	goes to and returns from a subroutine.
GoTo	goes to a specified line within a procedure.
If ... Then ... Else	runs different sets of statements according to a condition.
On ... GoSub	runs a subroutine according to the value of an expression.
On ... GoTo	goes to one of several specified lines.
Property Get	declares a **Property Get** procedure.
Property Let	declares a **Property Let** procedure.
Property Set	declares a **Property Set** procedure.
Select Case	runs different sets of statements according to the value of an expression.
Stop	suspends running the VBA code.
Sub ... End Sub	defines the beginning and end of a **Sub** procedure.
While ... Wend	repeats a block of statements while a condition is **True**.
With	runs a set of statements on an object.

3. Converting data

Functions

Asc()	returns the ASCII value of a character.
CBool()	converts an expression to a Boolean type.
CByte()	converts an expression to a Byte type.
CCur()	converts a string to a Currency type.
CDate()	converts an expression to a Date expression.
CDbl()	converts a string of number characters to double type.
CDec()	converts an expression to a Decimal type.
Chr()	returns the ASCII character corresponding to an ASCII code.
CInt()	converts a string to an integer number type.
CLng()	converts a string to a long number type.
CSng()	converts a string to a single number type.
CStr()	converts an expression to string format.
CVar()	converts a string to a variant type number.
CVErr()	returns a code specified by the user.
DateSerial()	returns a date number for a specified year, month and day.
DateValue()	converts a string expression to a date.
Day()	returns the day of the month in a date.
Hex()	converts a number to its hexadecimal equivalent as a string.

Oct()	converts a number to its octal equivalent as a string.
Str()	converts a number to a string.
Val()	converts a string to a number.

4. Date and time

Functions

Date()	returns the current date and time.
DateAdd()	adds an interval to a date.
DateDiff()	returns the difference between two dates.
DatePart()	extracts part of a date.
DateSerial()	returns the date corresponding to a year, month and day.
DateValue()	returns the date corresponding to a string.
Day()	returns the day in the month (1 to 31) for a specified time expression.
Hour()	returns the hour in the day (0 to 23) for a specified time expression.
IsDate()	indicates if you can convert a specified Variant into a date.
Minute()	returns the minute in the hour (0 to 59) for a specified time expression.
Month()	returns the month (1 to 12) for a specified time expression.

Now()	returns the current date and time.
Second()	returns the second in the minute (0 to 59) for a specified time expression.
Time()	returns the current system time.
Timer()	returns the number of seconds elapsed since midnight.
TimeSerial()	returns the serial time corresponding to a specified hour, minute and second.
TimeValue()	returns the time corresponding to a specified string.
WeekDay()	returns the day of the week corresponding to a time expression.
Year()	returns the year value corresponding to a date.

Statements

Date	sets the current date.
Time	sets the current time.

5. Declarations

Statements

Const	sets a symbolic constant.
Declare	declares a DLL subroutine.
Deftype	defines a default type.
Dim	defines a variable.

Let	assigns a value to a variable.
Option Base	defines the smallest value of an array index.
Option Compare	defines the compare mode between text files.
Option Explicit	forces the programmer to declare variables explicitly.
Option Private Module	forbids external references to the contents of a module.
Private	defines a private variable or a procedure.
Public	defines a public variable or a procedure.
ReDim	resizes a dynamic array.
Set	assigns an object to a variable.
Static	defines a static variable.
Type	defines a structured user variable.

6. Domains

Functions

DAvg()	calculates the average of a set of records (domain).
DCount()	counts the number of records in a domain.
DFirst()	returns the first record in a domain.
DLast()	returns the last record in a domain.
DLookUp()	searches in a domain.
DMax()	returns the maximum value in a domain according to specified criteria.

DMin()	returns the minimum value in a domain according to specified criteria.
DStDev()	calculates the standard deviation in a population sample.
DStDevP()	calculates the standard deviation in a population.
DSum()	calculates the sum of a set of values in a domain.
DVar()	calculates the variance in a population sample.
DVarP()	calculates the variance in a population.

7. Dynamic data exchange

Functions

DDE()	sets up a DDE channel and requests information.
DDEInitiate()	begins a conversation via a DDE channel.
DDERequest()	requests an item of information via a DDE channel.
DDESend()	sends an item of information via a DDE channel.

Statements

DDEExecute	uses an open DDE channel to send a command to an application.
DDEPoke	uses an open DDE channel to send data to an application.
DDETerminate	closes a DDE channel.
DDETerminate All	closes all open DDE channels.

8. File input/output

Functions

CurDir()	returns the current path.
Dir()	finds files and folders corresponding to a path and a name pattern.
EOF()	indicates whether or not the current record is at the end of the file.
FileAttr()	indicates the file mode for an open file.
FileDateTime()	indicates the date and time a file was created or last modified.
FileLen()	returns the length of a file.
FreeFile()	returns the next available file number.
GetAttr()	returns the attributes of a file or a folder.
Loc()	returns the current read/write position in a file.
LOF()	returns the length of a file.
Seek()	returns the current read/write position in a file.
Spc()	inserts spaces to position output in a Print statement.
Tab()	inserts tabs to position output in a Print statement.

Statements

ChDir	changes the current folder.
ChDrive	changes the current drive.
Close	closes a file.

FileCopy	copies a file.
Get	gets data from a sequential file.
Input	reads data from a sequential file.
Kill	deletes files on the hard disk.
Line Input	reads a line from a sequential file.
Lock	locks a file segment to stop users accessing it.
MkDir	creates a folder.
Name	assigns a new name to a disk file.
Open	opens a file.
Print	writes data to a sequential file.
Put	writes a variable to a file.
Reset	closes all open files.
RmDir	deletes a folder.
SetAttr	changes the attributes of a file.
Unlock	unlocks a file segment so that other users can access it.
Width	assigns an output line width for a sequential file.
Write	writes data to a sequential file.

9. Finance

Functions

DDB() returns the depreciation for an asset for a specified period of time using a double-declining balance method or another method.

FV() returns the future value of an annuity for a set of periodic fixed payments and a fixed interest rate.

IPmt() returns the interest payment for a set of periodic fixed payments and a fixed interest rate.

IRR() returns the internal rate of return for a set of payments and receipts.

MIRR() returns the modified internal rate of return for a set of payments and receipts.

NPer() returns the number of periods for a set of fixed payments and a fixed interest rate.

NPV() returns the net present value of an investment for a set of payments and receipts and a discount rate.

Pmt() returns the payment for an annuity based on a set of periodic fixed payments and a fixed interest rate.

PPmt() returns the principal payment for an annuity based on a set of periodic fixed payments and a fixed interest rate.

PV() returns the present value for an annuity based on a set of periodic fixed payments and a fixed interest rate.

RATE() returns the interest rate per period for an annuity.

SLN()	returns the straight-line depreciation for an asset for a determined period.
SYD()	returns the sum-of-years' digit depreciation for an asset for a period.

10. Error management

Functions

CVErr()	returns an error variable.
Err()	returns an error code as an integer.
Error()	returns the standard message corresponding to an error number.
IsError()	indicates if an expression is an error value.

Statements

Error	simulates an error.
On Error	specifies an action in the event of an error.
Resume	specifies an action following the processing of an error.

11. Graphics for reports

Functions

QBColor() returns the RGB color code for a specified color number.

RGB() returns an RGB color as a long integer.

12. Object referencing and embedding

Functions

CreateObject() creates and returns an ActiveX object reference.

GetObject() returns an object reference provided by an ActiveX component.

13. Handling objects

Methods

CreateControl creates a control in an open form.

CreateForm creates a form.

CreateReport creates a report.

CreateReportControl creates a control in an open report.

DeleteControl deletes a form control.

DeleteReportControl deletes a report control.

14.Mathematics

Functions

Abs()	returns the absolute value of a number.
Atn()	returns the arctangent of a number.
Cos()	returns the cosine of an angle in radians.
Exp()	returns an exponential.
Fix()	returns the integer part of a number: for negative number, it returns the first negative integer number that is greater than or equal to the number.
Int()	returns the integer part of a number: for negative number, it returns the first negative integer number that is less than or equal to the number.
Log()	returns the natural logarithm for a number.
Rnd()	returns a random number.
Sgn()	returns the sign of a number.
Sin()	returns the sine of an angle in radians.
Sqr()	returns the square root of a number.
Tan()	returns the tangent of an angle in radians.

Statements

Randomize	initialize the random number generator.

15.SQL

Functions

Avg()	calculates the average value of a field for a set of records.
Count()	counts the number of records (controls or SQL expressions).
First()	returns the value of a field in the first record in a query, a form or a report.
Last()	returns the value of a field in the last record in a query, a form or a report.
Max()	returns the maximum value of a field in a set of records.
Min()	returns the minimum value of a field in a set of records.
StDev(), StDevP()	estimates the standard deviation in a population sample or a population.
Sum()	returns the sum of the values in a field in a set of records.
Var(), VarP()	calculates the variance in a population sample or a population.

16.Arrays

Functions

IsArray() returns a Boolean value that indicates whether or not a variable is an array.

Array() returns a Variant value containing an array.

Statements

Erase reinitializes a static array and frees dynamic array storage space.

LBound, UBound returns the smallest or largest available subscript for an array dimension.

Option Base sets the lower bound for array subscripts.

ReDim dynamically resizes an array.

17.Checking variables

Functions

IsDate() indicates whether or not an expression can be converted to a date.

IsEmpty() indicates whether or not a variable is empty.

IsMissing() indicates whether or not an optional argument has been passed to a procedure.

IsNull() indicates whether or not a variable is null (does not contain valid data).

IsNumeric() indicates whether or not a variable is numeric.

IsObject() indicates whether or not an expression refers to an object.

TypeName() returns a string indicating the type of a variable.

VarType() indicates the source data type of a variant type variable.

18.Miscellaneous

Functions

Command() returns the argument part of the command line that started Microsoft Access.

CreateGroupLevel() creates a group level in a report.

CurrentUser() returns the name of the user who is currently logged on.

DoEvents() yields the processor to allow Windows to process other events.

Environ() returns the sting associated with an environment variable.

GetAllSettings() returns the names and values of the keys from an application's entry in the Windows registry.

GetSetting() returns a key value from an application's entry in the Windows registry.

InputBox()	displays a prompt in a dialog box then returns the contents of the text box as a string.
MsgBox()	displays a message box.
Shell()	runs a program.
StrReverse()	returns the specified string in reverse order.

Statements

AppActivate	activates a Windows application window.
Beep	emits a tone.
SendKeys	sends a sequence of keystrokes to the active window.
DeleteSetting	deletes a section or a key setting from an application's entry in the Windows registry.
Rem	allows you to include remarks in a program.
SaveSetting	saves or creates an application entry in the Windows registry.

19.Trappable error codes

Errors can occur when you are developing, compiling or running an application. You can test and respond to trappable errors using the **On Error** statement and the **Err** object.

Code	Error Description
3	Return without GoSub.
5	Invalid procedure call.
6	Overflow.

7	Out of memory.
9	Subscript out of range.
10	This array is fixed or temporarily locked.
11	Division by zero.
13	Type mismatch.
14	Out of string space.
16	Expression too complex.
17	Can't perform requested operation.
18	User interrupt occurred.
20	Resume without error.
28	Out of stack space.
35	Sub, Function, or Property not defined.
47	Too many DLL application clients.
48	Error in loading DLL.
49	Bad DLL calling convention.
51	Internal error.
52	Bad file name or number.
53	File not found.
54	Bad file mode.
55	File already open.
57	Device I/O error.
58	File already exists.
59	Bad record length.

61	Disk full.
62	Input past end of file.
63	Bad record number.
67	Too many files.
68	Device unavailable.
70	Permission denied.
71	Disk not ready.
74	Can't rename with different drive.
75	Path/File access error.
76	Path not found.
91	Object variable or With block variable not set.
92	For loop not initialized.
93	Invalid pattern string.
94	Invalid use of Null.
97	Can't call Friend procedure on an object that is not an instance of the defining class.
98	A property or method call cannot include a reference to a private object, either as an argument or as a return value.
298	System DLL could not be loaded.
320	Can not use character device names in specified file names.
321	Invalid file format.
322	Can't create necessary temporary file.

325	Invalid format in resource file.
327	Data value named not found.
328	Illegal parameter; can't write arrays.
335	Could not access system registry.
336	ActiveX component not correctly registered.
337	ActiveX component not found.
338	ActiveX component did not run correctly.
360	Object already loaded.
361	Can't load or unload this object.
363	ActiveX control specified not found.
364	Object was unloaded.
365	Unable to unload within this context.
368	The specified file is out of date. This program requires a later version.
371	The specified object can't be used as an owner form for Show.
380	Invalid property value.
381	Invalid property-array index.
382	Property Set can't be executed at run time.
383	Property Set can't be used with a read-only property.
385	Need property-array index.
387	Property Set not permitted.
393	Property Get can't be executed at run time.
394	Property Get can't be executed on write-only property.

400	Form already displayed; can't show modally.
402	Code must close topmost modal form first.
419	Permission to use object denied.
422	Property not found.
423	Property or method not found.
424	Object required.
425	Invalid object use.
429	ActiveX component can't create object or return reference to this object.
430	Class doesn't support Automation.
432	File name or class name not found during Automation operation.
438	Object doesn't support this property or method.
440	Automation error.
442	Connection to type library or object library for remote process has been lost.
443	Automation object doesn't have a default value.
445	Object doesn't support this action.
446	Object doesn't support named arguments.
447	Object doesn't support current locale setting.
448	Named argument not found.
449	Argument not optional or invalid property assignment.
450	Wrong number of arguments or invalid property assignment.

451	Object not a collection.
452	Invalid ordinal.
453	Specified DLL function not found.
454	Code resource not found.
455	Code resource lock error.
457	This key is already associated with an element of this collection.
458	Variable uses a type not supported in Visual Basic.
459	This component doesn't support the set of events.
460	Invalid Clipboard format.
461	Specified format doesn't match format of data.
462	The remote server machine does not exist or is unavailable.
463	Class not registered on local machine.
480	Can't create AutoRedraw image.
481	Invalid picture.
482	Printer error.
483	Printer driver does not support specified property.
484	Problem getting printer information from the system. Make sure the printer is set up correctly.
485	Invalid picture type.
486	Can't print form image to this type of printer.
520	Can't empty Clipboard.
521	Can't open Clipboard.

735	Can't save file to TEMP directory.
744	Search text not found.
746	Replacements too long.
31001	Out of memory.
31004	No object.
31018	Class is not set.
31027	Unable to activate object.
31032	Unable to create embedded object.
31036	Error saving to file.
31037	Error loading from file.

B. VBA constants

With VBA you can define constants to make your code more readable and easier to maintain.

You can also use the following VBA constants (intrinsic constants) anywhere in your code.

1. Color constants

Constant	Value	Description
vbBlack	0x0	Black
vbRed	0xFF	Red
vbGreen	0xFF00	Green
vbYellow	0xFFFF	Yellow
vbBlue	0x0FF0000	Blue
vbMagenta	0x0FF00FF	Magenta
vbCyan	0x0FFFF00	Cyan
vbWhite	0x0FFFFFF	White

2. Day constants

Constant	Value	Description
vbSunday	1	Sunday
vbMonday	2	Monday
vbTuesday	3	Tuesday
vbWednesday	4	Wednesday
vbThursday	5	Thursday
vbFriday	6	Friday

Constant	Value	Description
vbSaturday	7	Saturday

3. Keyboard constants

The constant values of the A to Z keys correspond to the ASCII codes for these characters.

Constant	Value	Description
vbKeyA	65	A key
vbKeyB	66	B key
vbKeyC	67	C key
...	...	...
vbKeyZ	90	Z key

The constant values of the 0 to 9 keys correspond to the ASCII codes for these characters.

Constant	Value	Description
vbKey0	48	0 key
vbKey1	49	1 key
vbKey2	50	2 key
...	...	...

Constant	Value	Description
vbKey9	57	9 key

4. Function key constants

Constant	Value	Description
vbKeyF1	0x70	F1 key
vbKeyF2	0x71	F2 key
...	...	...
vbKeyF11	0x7A	F11 key
...	...	...
vbKeyF16	0x7F	F16 key

5. Other key constants

Constant	Value	Description
vbKeyCancel	0x3	Esc key
vbKeyBack	0x8	← key
vbKeyTab	0x9	⇄ key

Constant	Value	Description
vbKeyClear	0xC	**Clear** key
vbKeyReturn	0xD	Enter key
vbKeyShift	0x10	⇧ Shift key
vbKeyControl	0x11	Ctrl key
vbKeyMenu	0x12	**MENU** key
vbKeyPause	0x13	Break key
vbKeyCapital	0x14	Caps Lock key
vbKeyEscape	0x1B	Esc key
vbKeySpace	0x20	space key
vbKeyPageUp	0x21	Pg Up key
vbKeyPageDown	0x22	Pg Dn key
vbKeyEnd	0x23	End key
vbKeyHome	0x24	Home key
vbKeyLeft	0x25	← key
vbKeyUp	0x26	↑ key
vbKeyRight	0x27	→ key
vbKeyDown	0x28	↓ key

Constant	Value	Description
vbKeySelect	0x29	**Select** key
vbKeyPrint	0x2A	**Print** key
vbKeyExecute	0x2B	**Execute** key
vbKeySnapshot	0x2C	**Snapshot** key
vbKeyInsert	0x2D	[Inser] key
vbKeyDelete	0x2E	[Del] key
vbKeyHelp	0x2F	**Help** key
vbKeyNumlock	0x90	[⊖] key
vbKeyLButton	0x1	Left mouse button
vbKeyRButton	0x2	Right mouse button

C. Shortcut keys

[F1] provides help on the selected keyword.

[F5] runs a procedure.

[F8] switches to step into (single step) mode.

[⇧Shift] [F8] switches to step over mode.

Ctrl + Shift + F8	switches to step out mode.
Ctrl + F8	runs to current cursor position.
Shift + F9	displays current value.
F9	sets or clears a breakpoint.
Ctrl + Shift + F9	clears all breakpoints.
Ctrl + F9	sets next statement.

A

D

E

F

K

L

M

N

O

P

Q

R

S

T

U

V

W

X

ISBN	TITLE	AUTHOR	PRICE	PAGES
8131800377	**Fundamentals of Information Technology Including MS Office**	Dinesh Maidasani, Jai Narayan Yadav	Rs. 175.00	356
813180089X	**Fundamentals of Information Technology Including MS Office (Hindi Medium)**	Dinesh Maidasani, Jai Narayan Yadav	Rs. 175.00	425
8170089719	**Foundations of Computer Science**	Ashok Arora	Rs. 250.00	386

CALL CENTERS

ISBN	TITLE	AUTHOR	PRICE	PAGES
8170082196	**Call Centers Made Easy**	Stephen Medcroft	Rs. 195.00	310

CISCO

ISBN	TITLE	AUTHOR	PRICE	PAGES
8170087481	**Enabling IP Routing with Cisco Routers**	R. Das, K. Chakrabarty	Rs. 295.00	486
817008749X	**Designing Networks with Cisco**	H. Pasricha, D. Jagu	Rs. 195.00	316
8170087503	**Cisco IP Routing Protocols: Troubleshooting Techniques**	V. Anand, K. Chakrabarty	Rs. 295.00	409

DATABASES

ISBN	TITLE	AUTHOR	PRICE	PAGES
8170089530	**DBMS—Complete Practical Approach**	Sharad Maheshwari, Ruchin Jain	Rs. 350.00	656
8170082404	**Learn to Program Visual Basic-Examples**	John Smiley	Rs. 295.00	482
8170082412	**Learn to Program Visual Basic-Databases**	John Smiley	Rs. 325.00	653
8170082420	**Learn to Program Visual Basic-Objects**	John Smiley	Rs. 325.00	670
817008475X	**IT Resources-Access 2002 VBA Programming Access**	Michele Amelot	Rs. 195.00	424
8170084512	**The Power of Oracle 9i**	Rajiv Parida, Vinod Sharma	Rs. 475.00	1035
8170088518	**Principles and Implementation of Data Warehousing**	Rajiv A. Parida	Rs. 295.00	487
817008864X	**DBA Study Guide OCP Prep Guide**	Nazar Abdul	Rs. 295.00	474
8170088658	**Oracle 11i—The Complete Reference**	Rashmi Anandi	Rs. 495.00	975
8131800067	**Toxonomy of Database Management System**	Aditya Kumar Gupta	Rs. 75.00	146
8131800385	**Introduction to SQL and PL/SQL**	Sharad Maheshwari, Ruchin Jain	Rs. 200.00	389

ISBN	TITLE	AUTHOR	PRICE	PAGES
	DOEACC 'O' LEVEL			
8170088089	**DOEACC 'O' Level Model Test Papers**	Ramesh Bangia	Rs. 175.00	296
8170089115	**DOEACC 'O' & 'A' Level Programming & Problem Solving Through 'C' Language (Model Test Paper with Solutions)**	Mukesh Sharma	Rs. 95.00	213
8170089069	**DOEACC 'O' & 'A' Level Business Systems (Model Test Paper with Solutions)**	Mukesh Sharma	Rs. 100.00	252
8170085640	**Programming and Problem Solving Through "C" Language**	Harsha Priya, R. Ranjeet	Rs. 95.00	306
8170084474	**IT Tools and Applications**	Ramesh Bangia	Rs. 145.00	370
8170085594	**Business Systems**	Ramesh Bangia	Rs. 175.00	452
8170089514	**Internet &Web Design**	Ramesh Bangia	Rs. 150.00	300
	ELECTRONIC COMMERCE			
8170085497	**Electronic Commerce**	Pete Loshin, John Vacca	Rs. 295.00	472
817008119X	**E-Commerce**	Mamta Bhusry	Rs. 95.00	215
8170083524	**Marketing in the Cyber Age**	Kurt Rohner	Rs. 295.00	223
	HARDWARE/EMBEDDED SYSTEMS			
8170087473	**Essential Electronics for PC Technicians**	John W. Farber	Rs. 295.00	546
8170086264	**Grid Computing: A Practical Guide to Technology and Applications**	Ahmar Abbas	Rs. 295.00	408
8170088186	**CD Cracking Uncovered Protection Against Unsanctioned CD Copy**	Kris Kaspersky	Rs. 295.00	422
8170083435	**Practical Linux Programming: Device Drivers, Embedded Systems and the Internet**	Ashfaq A. Khan	Rs. 295.00	420
8170083575	**TCP/IP Application Layer Protocols for Embedded Systems**	M. Tim Jones	Rs. 295.00	460
8131800520	**PC Repair and Maintenance : A Practical Guide**	Joel Rosenthal, Kevin Irwin	Rs. 195.00	362

ISBN	TITLE	AUTHOR	PRICE	PAGES
8131800768	**The A+ Certification and PC Repair Handbook**	Christopher A Crayton, Joel Z. Rosenthal	Rs. 495.00	888

INTERNET & WEB TECHNOLOGY

ISBN	TITLE	AUTHOR	PRICE	PAGES
8170083206	**The Internet Handbook for Writers, Students and Teachers**	Mary McGuire, Linda Stilborne	Rs. 195.00	276
8170084776	**Way in-Internet Getting Started**	Elizabeth Bramire	Rs. 95.00	165
8170088976	**Web Technology**	Ramesh Bangia	Rs. 250.00	560
8170087163	**Web Design with Macromedia Studio MX 2004**	Eric Hunley	Rs. 295.00	558
8170083400	**Professional Web Design (Techniques and Templates)**	Clint Eccher	Rs. 295.00	425
8170088046	**HTML, XHTML, CSS and XML**	Teodoru Gugoiu	Rs. 195.00	355
8170083583	**FrontPage 2000 for Visual Learners**	Chris Charuhas	Rs. 95.00	200
8170083591	**HTML & Java Script for Visual Learners**	Chris Charuhas	Rs. 95.00	200
8170083605	**The Visual Learners Guide to Managing Web Projects**	Chris Charuhas	Rs. 95.00	130
8170083613	**Dreamweaver 4 for Visual Learners**	Chris Charuhas	Rs. 95.00	200
8170084768	**IT Resource-Implementing XML: Managing and Formatting Data**	Johhny Brochard	Rs. 125.00	279
8170089476	**Design Your Web World**	Sunil Jalota	Rs. 75.00	146

KEEPING AHEAD SERIES

ISBN	TITLE	AUTHOR	PRICE	PAGES
8170084652	**Keeping Ahead-Exchange 2000 Server**	Philippe Levesque	Rs. 145.00	285
8170084660	**Keeping Ahead-Windows 2000 Professional**	Jose Dardoigne	Rs. 175.00	388
8170084679	**Keeping Ahead-Windows 2000 Server**	Philippe Mathon	Rs. 175.00	360
8170084687	**Keeping Ahead-Linux Administration Kernel Version 2.0 to 2.2**	Bruno Guèrin	Rs. 125.00	240

Please write for a free color Firewall Media Catalog for details on the above books.

ISBN	TITLE	AUTHOR	PRICE	PAGES
8170084695	**Keeping Ahead-Using Linux Kernel Version 2.0 to 2.2**	Bruno Guèrin	Rs. 125.00	258
8170084709	**Keeping Ahead-Java 2**	Benjamin Aumaille	Rs. 145.00	284
8170084717	**Keeping Ahead-SQL Server 7**	Joelle Mosset	Rs. 145.00	329
8170084725	**Keeping Ahead-JavaScript and VBScript**	Benjamin Aumaille	Rs. 145.00	313
8170084733	**Keeping Ahead-C++ Programming Language**	Bruno Dubois	Rs. 125.00	234
8170084741	**Keeping Ahead-TCP/IP in the NT Environment**	Bruno Ferec	Rs. 125.00	230

MCSE

ISBN	TITLE	AUTHOR	PRICE	PAGES
817008489X	**MCSE-Administering SQL Server 7.0**	Jerome Gabillaud	Rs. 295.00	580
8170084903	**MCSE-Networking Essentials**	Jose Dordoigne	Rs. 245.00	453
8170084911	**MCSE-Windows 2000 Professional**	Jose Dordoigne	Rs. 325.00	665
817008492X	**MCSE-Windows 2000 Server**	Phillippe Mathon	Rs. 345.00	712

MULTIMEDIA AND ANIMATION

ISBN	TITLE	AUTHOR	PRICE	PAGES
8170088208	**3DS Max 6 Animation with Character Studio 4 and Plug-Ins**	Boris Kulagin, Dmitry Morozov	Rs. 175.00	216
8170088216	**Adobe Audition: Soundtracks for Digital Video**	Roman Petelin, Yury Petelin	Rs. 195.00	278
8170086205	**Building A Digital Human**	Ken Brilliant	Rs. 295.00	380
8170086213	**Making Digital Videos**	Ben Long	Rs. 295.00	284
8170087171	**Illustrating with Macromedia Flash ™ MX2004**	Robert Firbaugh	Rs. 245.00	366
8170082439	**Multimedia Basics-Technology (Vol. I)**	Andreas Holzinger	Rs. 195.00	312
8170082447	**Multimedia Basics-Learning (Vol. II)**	Andreas Holzinger	Rs. 195.00	326
8170082455	**Multimedia Basics-Design (Vol. III)**	Andreas Holzinger	Rs. 195.00	280
8170083532	**Maya Feature Creature Creations**	Todd Palamar	Rs. 295.00	376

Please write for a free color Firewall Media Catalog for details on the above books.

ISBN	TITLE	AUTHOR	PRICE	PAGES
8170083540	**Sound Forge Power**	Scott R. Garrigus	Rs. 195.00	344
8131800288	**Multimedia and Web Technology**	Ramesh Bangia	Rs. 395.00	878
813180044X	**Photoshop CS**	Shruti Lal	Rs. 195.00	434

NETWORKING

ISBN	TITLE	AUTHOR	PRICE	PAGES
817008721X	**Networking Essentials**	Jose Dordoigne	Rs. 195.00	453
8170089328	**TCP/IP Distributed System**	Vivek Acharya	Rs. 250.00	474
8170087023	**Computer Networks**	Ajit Kumar Singh	Rs. 95.00	181
8131800148	**The Real—world Network Troubleshooting Manual**	Alan Sugano	Rs. 295.00	396
817008203X	**Telecom & Networking Glossary**	Robert Mastin	Rs. 300.00	250
8170082048	**Data Networking Made Easy**	Karen Patten	Rs. 360.00	350
8170082056	**Digital Convergence**	Andy Covell	Rs. 300.00	234

OFFICE AUTOMATION

ISBN	TITLE	AUTHOR	PRICE	PAGES
8170089891	**Desk Top Publishing**	Dinesh Maidasani	Rs. 150.00	311
8170087805	**Learning Computer Fundamentals, MS Office and Internet & Web Technology**	Dinesh Maidasani	Rs. 95.00	301
8170087686	**MS-Word 2000 Thumb-Rules and Details**	Snigdha Banerjee	Rs. 175.00	390
8170089239	**Computer Accounting with Tally 7.2**	Firewall Media	Rs. 195.00	330

ON YOUR SIDE SERIES

ISBN	TITLE	AUTHOR	PRICE	PAGES
8170084830	**On your Side-Powerpoint 2002**	Andrew Blackburn	Rs. 145.00	282
8170084849	**On your Side-Excel 2002**	Adrienne Tommy	Rs. 125.00	275
8170084857	**On your Side-Word 2002**	Adrienne Tommy	Rs. 125.00	289
8170084865	**On your Side-Access 2002**	Adrienne Tommy	Rs. 125.00	303
8170084873	**On your Side-Frontpage 2002**	Andrew Blackburn	Rs. 95.00	245
8170084881	**On your Side-Windows XP**	Adrienne Tommy	Rs. 125.00	310

ISBN	TITLE	AUTHOR	PRICE	PAGES
	OPERATING SYSTEMS			
8170087236	**Linux—A Practical Approach**	B. Mohamed Ibrahim	Rs. 95.00	187
8170088623	**Red Hat Linux Study Guide**	Vijay Shekhar	Rs. 350.00	635
8170088631	**Red Hat Linux-The Complete Bible**	Vijay Shekhar	Rs. 545.00	1176
8170089581	**Unix and Shell Programming**	Archana Verma	Rs. 80.00	137
8170089131	**Operating System Concepts**	P.S. Gill	Rs. 95.00	181
8170083427	**The MS-Windows XP Professional Handbook**	Louis Columbus	Rs. 295.00	330
8170084784	**Way in-Windows XP Home Edition**	Andrew Blackburn	Rs. 95.00	183
8170086221	**Cyber Rookies—Operating System Fundamentals**	D. Irtegov	Rs. 295.00	498
	PROGRAMMING			
8170087791	**The Art of Programming Through Flowcharts & Algorithms**	Anil Bikas Chaudhuri	Rs. 95.00	160
8170086248	**Preventative Programming Techniques: Avoid and Correct Common Mistakes**	Brian Hawkins	Rs. 295.00	322
8170083443	**Learning Computer Programming : It's not about Languages**	Mary Farrell	Rs. 295.00	375
8170086256	**Object-Oriented Programming: From Problem Solving to Java**	José M. Garrido	Rs. 295.00	360
817008931X	**Object-Oriented Programming-Concept and Implementation**	A. Rajesh	Rs. 95.00	182
8170089107	**Java: J2SE-5 A Practical Approach**	B. Mohammad Ibrahim	Rs. 175.00	332
8170089409	**Advance Java**	Gajendra Gupta	Rs. 175.00	305
8170088038	**Assembly Language Programming for Intel Processors Family**	Vasile Lungu	Rs. 295.00	577
8170088178	**The Assembly Programming Master Book**	Vlad Pirogov	Rs. 395.00	726
813180075X	**Java Messaging**	Eric Bruno	Rs. 295.00	480

ISBN	TITLE	AUTHOR	PRICE	PAGES

PROGRAMMING - C#, C, C++

8170083702	**The Power of C#**	Rajiv Parida	Rs. 295.00	576
8170085632	**Mastering Graphics Programming in 'C'**	Sudhir Dawra	Rs. 145.00	286
8170088879	**Programming in C and Numerical Analysis**	J.B. Dixit	Rs. 350.00	355
8170087074	**Mastering C Programs**	J.B. Dixit	Rs. 195.00	434
8170081262	**Programming in C**	J.B. Dixit	Rs. 295.00	506
8170087619	**Unix and C Programming**	Ashok Arora, Shefali Bansal	Rs. 295.00	606
817008878X	**C Interview Questions and Answers**	J. Rajaram	Rs. 75.00	139
8170089034	**Pragmatic C**	R.K. Jangda	Rs. 150.00	258
8170086140	**Data Structure for 'C' Programming**	Ajay Kumar	Rs. 145.00	290
8170081270	**Programming in C++**	J.B. Dixit	Rs. 260.00	602
8170088194	**Hackish C++ Pranks & Tricks**	Michael Flenov	Rs. 245.00	326
8170082889	**Basics of C++ Programming**	Nishant Kundalia	Rs. 95.00	168
8170083648	**Mastering C++ Programs**	J.B. Dixit	Rs. 295.00	598
817008623X	**Cyber Rookies—C++ Programming Fundamentals**	Chuck Easttom	Rs. 295.00	417
8131800202	**Data Structure using C++**	N. Jayalakshmi	Rs. 65.00	126
8170089123	**C++ Made Easy**	T.D. Malhotra	Rs. 250.00	449
8131800393	**C++ & Introduction to C#**	T.D. Malhotra, Rajeev A. Parida, A. Rajesh	Rs. 200.00	440
8131800350	**OOPS with C++**	M. Jaya Prasad	Rs. 150.00	317

SECURITY

8170083419	**Computer Forensics : Computer Crime Scene Investigation**	John Vacca	Rs. 445.00	731
8131800156	**Computer Evidence (Collection and Preservation)**	Christopher L.T. Brown	Rs. 295.00	394
8170083494	**Firewall Architecture for the Enterprise**	Norbert Pohlmann, Tim Crothers	Rs. 295.00	480
8170086272	**Net Spies**	Andrew Gauntlett	Rs. 195.00	210
3826607546	**Firewall Systems**	Norbert Pohlmann	Rs. 1630.00	544
8131800504	**Homeland Security Techniques and Technologies**	Jesus Mena	Rs. 295.00	346

Please write for a free color Firewall Media Catalog for details on the above books.

ISBN	TITLE	AUTHOR	PRICE	PAGES
	ENGINEERING AND TECHNOLOGY			
817008718X	**Human Aspects of Software Engineering**	James E. Tomayko, Orit Hazzan	Rs. 195.00	338
8131800032	**Management Information Systems**	Avdhesh Gupta, Anurag Malik	Rs. 195.00	400
8170087953	**Human Computer Interaction**	Rajendra Ranjan Kumar	Rs. 95.00	210
8170088097	**Structured System Analysis and Design**	Preeti Gupta	Rs. 125.00	192
817008802X	**Autocad 2005 for Engineers**	Ionel Simion	Rs. 175.00	271
8170088054	**Digital Signal Processing Fundamentals**	Ashfaq A. Khan	Rs. 295.00	391
8131800164	**Digital Communication System Using System VUE**	Dennis Silage	Rs. 295.00	365
8170089719	**Foundations of Computer Science**	Ashok Arora	Rs. 250.00	386
817008363X	**Practical Project Management**	Ivan Bayross	Rs. 195.00	342
8131800806	**Digital Signal Processing using MATLAB and Wavelets**	Michael Weeks	Rs. 350.00	452
8131800792	**Classical Electrodynamics**	Hans C. Dhanian	Rs. 395.00	620
8131800512	**The Software Vulnerability Guide**	Herbert H. Thompson, Scott G. Chase	Rs. 195.00	368
8131800776	**Robot Modelling and Kinematics**	Rachid Manseur	Rs. 295.00	380
8131800369	**System Software**	M. Joseph	Rs. 95.00	185
	STRAIGHT TO THE POINT SERIES			
8170084601	**STTP : Word 2002**	Corinne Hervo	Rs. 45.00	154
817008461X	**STTP : Excel 2002**	Corinne Hervo	Rs. 45.00	153
8170084628	**STTP : Dreamweaver 4**	Corinne Hervo	Rs. 45.00	135
8170084636	**STTP : Flash 5**	Corinne Hervo	Rs. 45.00	183
8170084644	**STTP : Photoshop 6**	Corinne Hervo	Rs. 45.00	152
817008881X	**STTP : MS Office 2000**	Dinesh Maidasani	Rs. 125.00	290
8170086100	**STTP : MS Office 2003**	Dinesh Maidasani	Rs. 145.00	288
8170087651	**STTP : MS Word 2003**	Firewall Media	Rs. 60.00	150
8170088011	**STTP : Photoshop CS**	Firewall Media	Rs. 60.00	150
8170088143	**STTP : MS Excel 2003**	Firewall Media	Rs. 60.00	150
8170088151	**STTP : CorelDraw 12**	Firewall Media	Rs. 60.00	150
8131800105	**STTP : 3ds MAX 7**	Dinesh Maidasani	Rs. 95.00	182

ISBN	TITLE	AUTHOR	PRICE	PAGES
8131800083	**STTP : Auto CAD 2006**	Dinesh Maidasani	Rs. 95.00	190
8131800245	**STTP : CorelDraw X3**	Dinesh Maidasani	Rs. 75.00	188
8131800253	**STTP : Dreamweaver 8**	Dinesh Maidasani	Rs. 75.00	148
8131800237	**STTP : Photoshop CS2**	Dinesh Maidasani	Rs. 75.00	172
8170088380	**STTP : Tally 7.2**	Firewall Media	Rs. 175.00	322
8131800091	**STTP : Flash 8**	Dinesh Maidasani	Rs. 95.00	180
8131800407	**STTP : My SQL 5.0**	Dinesh Maidasani	Rs. 85.00	166
8131800458	**STTP : Microsoft Power Point 2003**	Dinesh Maidasani	Rs. 75.00	142

STUDIO FACTORY

ISBN	TITLE	AUTHOR	PRICE	PAGES
8170084792	**Studio Factory—Photoshop 6**	Christophe Aubry	Rs. 175.00	364
8170084806	**Studio Factory—Flash 5**	Sami Ben Yahiya	Rs. 145.00	314
8170084814	**Studio Factory—Dreamweaver Ultradev 4**	Phillippe Chatellier	Rs. 95.00	240
8170084822	**Studio Factory—Dreamweaver 4**	Christophe Aubry	Rs. 175.00	373
8170087643	**Studio Factory—Dreamweaver MX**	Christophe Aubry	Rs. 195.00	407
8170087627	**Studio Factory—Flash MX**	Arnaud Blanche	Rs. 145.00	337
817008766X	**Studio Factory—Photoshop 7**	Cyril Guerin	Rs. 195.00	420

LAXMI PUBLICATIONS (P) LTD

113, Golden House, Daryaganj, New Delhi-110002

Phone : **011 - 43 53 25 00**

Fax : **011 - 43 53 25 28**

EMAIL : info@laxmipublications.com

Website : www.laxmipublications.com

BRANCHES

- 129/1, IIIrd Main Road, IX Cross, Chamrajpet, **Bangalore** (*Phone* : 080-26 61 15 61)
- 26, Damodaran Street, T. Nagar, **Chennai** (*Phone* : 044-24 34 47 26)
- 43/1394D, St. Benedict's Road, Ernakulam North, **Cochin** (*Phone* : 0484-239 70 04)
- Pan Bazar, Rani Bari, **Guwahati** (*Phones* : 0361-254 36 69, 251 38 81)
- 4-2-453, Ist Floor, Ramkote, **Hyderabad** (*Phone* : 040-24 75 02 47)
- Adda Tanda Chowk, N.D. 365, **Jalandhar City** (*Phone* : 0181-222 12 72)
- 106/A, Ist Floor, S.N. Banerjee Road, **Kolkata** (*Phones* : 033-22 27 37 73, 22 27 52 47)
- 18, Madan Mohan Malviya Marg, **Lucknow** (*Phone* : 0522-220 95 78)
- 142-C, Victor House, Ground Floor, N.M. Joshi Marg, Lower Parel (W), **Mumbai** (*Phones* : 022-24 91 54 15, 24 92 78 69)
- Radha Govind Street, Tharpagna, **Ranchi** (*Phone* : 0651-230 77 64)